On Grace and Goodwill

I can't say there's one perfect town in North Carolina, because there are so many I'm drawn to — Asheboro, where I grew up, will forever feel like home. Greensboro, my home now, has fantastic farmers markets and one of my favorite bakeries, Adrian and Adriana Haisu's Augustino Gusto, known for their tangy sourdough bread and warmhearted welcomes.

I settled right in to Sparta one weekend, where I had a fabulous lunch at La Mexicana Grill, and the owner, who had moved to North Carolina from Spain, and his wife, from Bolivia, popped over to my table during the busiest part of the day to make sure I was enjoying myself. I watched the couple move around the room, their attention focused on every diner.

I've got a soft spot for Lumberton, too, made all the more meaningful to me when Melvin Morris, an artist who served as a Marine and now owns Inner Peace Center for the Arts, proudly gave me a tour of his gallery. He pointed out all the works on display, but I had to ask about the 3-by-4-foot oil-and-acrylic painting on one wall, a powerful depiction of Montford Point recruits during the era of segregation. "That one is mine," Morris said modestly, and I understood then that he wanted the spotlight on his community of artists, not on himself, and I couldn't help but be filled with admiration.

All around North Carolina, I see evidence of grace and goodwill, of humanity.

In Hatteras, I bowed my head as the Rev. Richard Joyner, a pastor and founder of the Conetoe Family Life Center, gave a blessing for a gathering of generations of fishermen and farmers and we had lunch on the waterfront. I was there for the Day at the Docks celebration, a homecoming for islanders and a tribute to working watermen and -women.

Joyner was there as an extension of his community — he'd brought

you make my heart sing

ELIZABETH HUDSON

artwork by Laura D. Poss

Published by *Our State* magazine, Mann Media, Inc.
PO Box 4552, Greensboro, NC 27404
(800) 948-1409 | ourstate.com
Printed in the United States by LSC Communications

EDITOR: Katie Schanze
DESIGN DIRECTOR: Claudia Royston
ART DIRECTOR: Jason Chenier
EDITORIAL DESIGNERS: Erin LaBree, Hannah Wright

Library of Congress Control Number: 2022915542

SANDWICHES
DELI-STYLE
Grilled on rye bread and
served with chips and pickles.
REUBEN
Thin slices of Kahns finest
corned beef with sauerkraut,
swiss cheese and 1000 Island
dressing
CORNED BEEF
Tender slices cooked our own
(Swiss cheese 15¢ extra)
PASTRAMI
Smith-Corona

Contents

vegetables from the Family Life Center's garden and honey that he and the schoolchildren of Edgecombe County harvested, all for chefs to use during a seafood cook-off. He talked about the center's mission: quite simply, to make life better for his congregants, his friends, his neighbors, for everyone who calls Edgecombe County home.

All around North Carolina, I see evidence of this grace and goodwill, of an outward focus, of humanity.

On a visit to Tarboro last summer, I stopped for lunch at On the Square and, afterward, took a walk around the 45-block historic district. From Main Street, I was within steps of at least four churches — Calvary Episcopal, with its bountiful churchyard gardens; First Baptist; Howard Memorial Presbyterian; and St. James United Methodist — the divine spaces that we hold as most welcoming of all.

As I walked on, I was struck by the plethora of porches in this town. Every house I passed was fronted by an open porch, that bridge between inside and outside, an intentional communal space meant for family, for neighbors, and, perhaps most important, for strangers. Friendship begins there, right?

In North Carolina, I see porches like this — such a universal symbol of hospitality — everywhere. In my hometown of Asheboro. In Southport and New Bern. In Winston-Salem and Durham. In Mount Airy and Washington. And I can't help but hope: If we can build them to front our homes, to create an open space for strangers to become friends, we can surely build them to front our hearts and find ourselves that much closer to creating a better place to live. **OS**

Built to Last

In 1979, we moved from our small house in downtown Asheboro to our new home in the country, a two-story Cape Cod on a hill. It had a sunken den with wide wooden beams overhead, a wood-burning fireplace, and a two-car garage.

My dad never intended to park any cars in that garage and instead turned it into a workshop, something he'd wanted his whole life. He built a woodworking table to fit the space and set up sawhorses in the corners. Over the years, he outfitted his shop well, accumulating a band saw, a circular saw, a jigsaw, a scroll saw. He hung clamps and handsaws from pegs and balanced large sheets of lumber against the walls. He filled three metal toolboxes with screwdrivers and hammers and made weekly runs to Lowe's for yet another tool, another screw, another nail, more sandpaper. Nearly every weekend, my dad was in that garage, sawing and hammering, tinkering and puttering. Poring over plans that he found in woodworking magazines.

You never saw a man more satisfied than my dad when he dusted wood shavings from his pants and stamped his shoes on the mat before going into the house, leaving behind residual proof of accomplishment, of projects completed.

Back then, my parents embraced the early-American folk art that was so popular at the time — needlepoint samplers, Shaker stacking boxes — and my dad made wooden miniatures and cutouts reflective of that style. He created alphabet letters and blocks, wooden birds and birdhouses. He made rustic stools and benches, picture frames and chalkboards. Whirligigs with wooden propellers that twirled in the wind. Nothing fancy, but everything was solid. Built to last.

When you're young, you don't think about traits like permanence and endurance.

When you're young, you don't think about traits like permanence and endurance. You assume that what's here now — the red pickup in the driveway, the pie safe in the kitchen — will always be here.

One winter evening, my dad came home from work to tell my mom and me that his doctor was sending him to the hospital for emergency open-heart surgery. One of his heart valves, weakened by the rheumatic fever he'd had as a boy, was finally giving out. Not everything, it seems, is built to last.

He came home with a long, vertical scar in the middle of his chest and instructions for a two-month recuperation. If you've known someone who's had heart surgery, you know they can't lift heavy objects or drive a car. Which meant that, on Valentine's Day, my dad couldn't get to the store to buy my mother a card, a tradition they'd not missed since the day they married.

That day, though, my dad made his way to the garage. He moved slowly, carefully, and picked up the lightest piece of plywood he had. He cut out a long, vertical heart and painted it red. With chalk, he drew a smiling stick figure with arms wide open. *Happy Valentine,* he wrote. *I love you this much.*

My mom still has the heart, my dad's handwriting still intact. It's lasted for a long time.

I think it'll last forever. **OS**

Carolina Glee Club

On spring mornings, the welcome arrival of birds buoys the spirit.

Still dark at 6 a.m. when I take my short, mile-and-a-half walk beneath the budding red maples and sprouting Bradford pears of my neighborhood streets. Up ahead, a car with dimmed headlights stops and starts, flashing intermittent brake lights: The newspaper carrier is leaving the warmth of his car to hand-deliver the paper to the front doorsteps instead of pitching it from his window the way you might expect. At this early hour, I'm the only one who sees this act of kindness, and I wonder if he knows how much the residents here appreciate it, how there are neighbors who need the convenience of a newspaper delivered to the threshold of their door or the eave of their porch, a welcome arrival.

By the time I make my way back to the house, the darkness has lifted with the first hint of light in the sky. Occasionally, I'm rewarded with the reds and corals and pinks and apricot and cantaloupe of springtime sunrises, hues that emerge slowly and deepen into a brilliant swipe across the sky, but even on days when that doesn't happen, the feather in the cap of my morning is always — can't resist — the opening trills, the coos and chirrups and warbles and whistles of birdsong, notes that start slowly and swell into an ensemble, an a cappella performance that never fails to lift my mood, to buoy my spirit. A welcome arrival.

I pay attention to the birds.

A few years ago — and, oh, how I hate to bring this back up — in a photo essay in the pages of this magazine, I misidentified a picture of a common redheaded woodpecker by calling it a rare sighting of an endangered red-cockaded woodpecker. I promise you, my mistake did not go unnoticed, and within days, I was inundated with letters and corrective phone calls. Thankfully, most readers forgave me, but even now, I remain mortified by the error, and shortly after that mistake, I went out and bought myself a squirrel-proof, 10-pound-seed-capacity bird feeder, which I hung from a crookneck pole right outside my kitchen window.

I cannot imagine the landscape of our state without the spectacle of these birds.

Every morning, sausage in the skillet and scrambled eggs and buttered toast on my plate, I have breakfast and watch for the birds that also come to feast on sunflower chips and shelled peanuts at their feeder. On Sundays, when I have more time, I spread out a laminated, foldable field guide called *Birds of North Carolina*, identification for 157 songbirds, hummingbirds, woodpeckers, shorebirds, waterfowl, doves, and owls, and I take note of whatever lands here.

I've had a profusion of Carolina wrens, which I know from their cinnamon bellies, and tiny Carolina chickadees, which I love for their contrasting black caps and white cheeks. I've been visited by goldfinches and warblers, bluebirds and robins, nuthatches and catbirds, and, certainly, northern cardinals, both the brown females and the dazzling red males, and I cannot imagine the landscape of our state without the spectacle of these birds, without the honor of their presence.

On mornings when there are no birds, there's usually a hawk circling overhead, tracking something from the woods nearby, and I get anxious, awaiting their return. I think of what it must've been like 100 years ago, when the now-extinct Carolina parakeet, with its copious 14 tailfeathers, kept company with our avian entourage, and I worry that one day, I'll have missed my chance to finally see that red-cockaded woodpecker.

I hold out hope that one day it'll come, and I'll be grateful for such a welcome arrival. **Os**

A Time to Every Purpose

It is time now for egg salad with good mayonnaise, a little mustard, and a spoonful of sweet salad cubes (Mount Olive for me, please), and you certainly don't need a recipe for that, but it makes me happy that Mildred Council made sure to include one, easy enough for a light lunch, in her *Mama Dip's Family Cookbook*, and there's one in the Greensboro Junior League's 1978 *Out of Our League* cookbook, too, a classic hostess offering for an afternoon visit from a neighbor. You have time to make that pitcher of tea, now, don't you? And there is always time for a slice of lemon meringue pie.

It is time now for early morning trips to the farmers market for radishes and dandelion greens and turnips and asparagus, perfectly plump and heaped in mounds in the wooden bins; it is time to fill our jam jars, our vases, our buckets with bunches of apricot tulips, pink peonies, lavender sweet pea, delicate colors that ease us gently into this fresh new season.

At home, my daffodils, fingerling size just a month ago, are finally full-legged and upright, emerged from their winter hibernation alive and awake, and seeing all of this — the outstretched arms of budding dogwoods; the green shoots of grass, reaching for the sun — makes me feel alive and awake, too, nudged, finally, by the arrival of spring.

Budding dogwoods and green shoots of grass make me feel alive, too, nudged by the arrival of spring.

We've been waiting all this time.

It's time now for grand openings: open all the windows to air out the house, to let in the sound of birdsong, of wind chimes dangling from the eaves of the porch; opening day at the baseball stadiums for the Down East Wood Ducks, for the Durham Bulls, for the Asheville Tourists; open the cover on the backyard grill for barbecued chicken, sticky with sauce; open the shed to check the lawnmower; open the cedar chest to store winter's blankets and shake out the log cabin-patterned quilt, the Carolina Lily quilt, heirlooms now, but their colors — remarkable, after all this time — still dazzle. Open the earth with the weeder, the digger, the tiller to ready a spot for summer's squash and tomatoes, for golden marigolds.

It's the season to find the open fields, the pastures, the meadows with patches of clover, soft and cool on bare feet. My aunt Joanna, an artist, had an amazing ability to find four-leaf clovers, which she'd pluck and hand to me to press between book pages, a gift to discover years later, long past the time when I'd forgotten they were there.

I think of pulling books from the shelves and opening, randomly, to see what treasures appear. An inscription, in my grandmother's looping cursive; an underlined passage of a poem; a recipe notation from my dad — "add more cocoa" or "good!" — memories of time spent with people I've loved.

And my heart opens with joy. **Os**

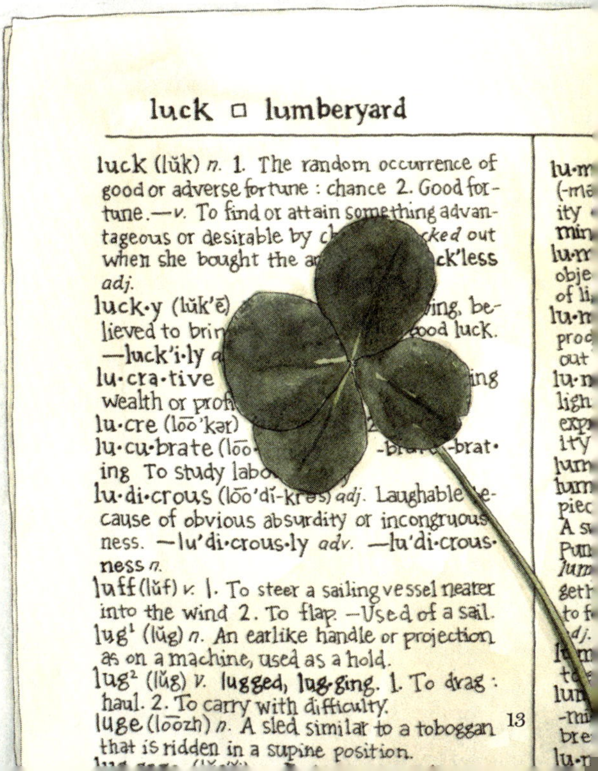

One-Hit Wonder

Several years ago, a reader sent me a Victorinox Swiss Army serrated tomato knife in the mail. It's got a red handle and stands out among all the other knives in my kitchen utensil drawer. I use it nearly every day in the summer, but only to slice tomatoes, its intended purpose, for the sandwiches I practically live off of, and every time, I think of the kindness of someone I only know through the pages of *Our State*.

In the era of multitasking, I prefer a single-purpose gadget. It's an appreciation I probably got from my dad.

He was a gadget man.

Oh, I wish you could've seen all the kitchen utensils my dad had, lined up so neatly in our drawers. He had a tool for everything: the two-sided melon baller, although we only ever sliced cantaloupe and watermelon into wedges; the wire egg slicer that cut hard-boiled eggs into 1/8-inch strips; an assortment of wooden-handled potato mashers; the garlic press; the butter molds; the strawberry-stem remover, skewers, graters, and a pasta maker that sat on top of the counter, although, like that melon baller, he never used it. I only ever saw the blue Mueller's box in our house, its recipe for "Classic Lasagne" torn from the back of the box and taped to the inside of the cabinet door.

Now *that* sandwich was a production, and I loved to watch my dad assemble it, the same way every time.

We had a cheese slicer attached to a wooden cutting board and a handheld vegetable chopper — you pumped the handle with your palm and sharp blades in the glass jar cut up onions and carrots. We had a hand-crank ice crusher mounted to the side of the cabinet over the sink, and a Hamilton Beach DrinkMaster in mint green for my dad's milkshakes, always with Sealtest chocolate ice cream.

Some of my favorite gadgets (aside from that milkshake maker) were the corn holders he kept in a box and skewered to the ends of our corn on the cob in the summer. He had a box of bamboo ones from Reed Runners, a gift shop that was in Friendly Center in Greensboro for many years, and a set in the shape of miniature ears of corn, two stainless-steel picks on their ends. I remember my dad skewering a hot ear of corn on my plate for me and teaching me his trick of twirling the corn in a stick of butter, leaving a little valley in the top until my mother smoothed it back out with a butter knife.

He made sandwiches for my mom and me in the summertime — homemade egg salad, pimento cheese, BLTs. Now *that* sandwich was a production, and I loved to watch my dad assemble it, the same way every time. Bottom slice of bread, toasted, Merita Old-Fashioned White, slathered in mayonnaise. Three strips of bacon, Oscar Mayer, the only brand he'd consider buying. Next came tomatoes, picked that morning from his garden and still sun-warm — four slices, 1/8-inch thick, overlapping, salted and peppered. Crisp iceberg lettuce on top of all that, dried with a paper towel to keep the bread from getting soggy. A final smear of mayonnaise on the top piece of toasted bread and a cut straight down the center with a serrated bread knife. A purpose for everything.

And then my dad would slide our sandwiches over to my mom and me, smiling, satisfied with such a humble act — of caretaking, of providing — another purpose fulfilled. **Os**

Art Springs Eternal

Like the faithful return of spring, outdoor art stirs our hearts.

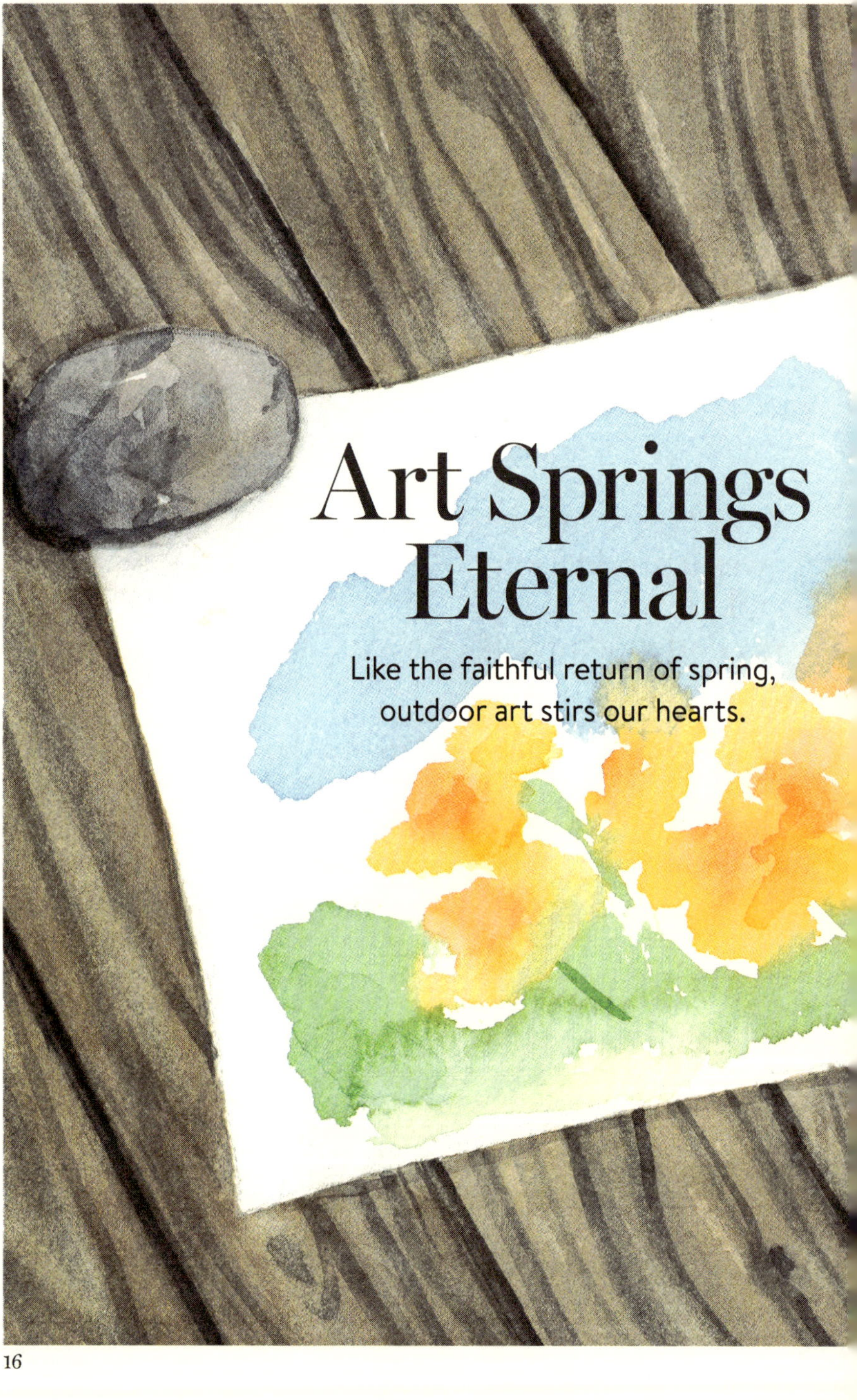

Finally, just when we thought we couldn't take winter much longer, spring sprung, making good on its promise once again. My grandmother traded the brocade drapes on her windows for airy sheers and laid a cotton braided rug over the hallway furnace vent. I traded my indoor coloring books for a drugstore watercolor paint set, the kind with two rows of colors and a red plastic paintbrush that snapped into the center of the tin.

While she went to the backyard to snip tulips, I found a spot in the sunshine on the front porch and carefully laid out my wares: my tin of paints, a stack of paper with a rock on top to guard against the wind, a jelly jar filled with water. I had no shortage of subjects for painting: yellow warblers that came to feed at my grandmother's bird feeder, tufts of green clover that sprouted all over the yard, golden stalks of forsythia that grew along the edge of the porch, daffodils that swayed in the flower beds, and a soft blue springtime sky hanging above it all.

Isn't this what art is meant to do? To stir a heart, to surprise. To pull light from the shadows.

I was content to stay on that porch all day, dabbing my brush into the oval pools of color, quietly creating my own little landscapes. I didn't realize that I was carrying on an *en plein air* tradition, the activity of painting outside popularized in the early 1800s. I just knew that the breeze dried my paints on the paper quicker, that colors showed up more vividly in the sunshine, and that, in the afternoon, my grandmother would join me to rock in her chair and smile as I showed her my work.

This year, spring fulfills its promise again — always, eternal — and although I no longer have that old drugstore pan of paints, I'll find a way to search for the art outside, to admire the masterpieces created by others.

I'll find one of those masterpieces on the grounds of Davidson College, in the soaring elm-and-sweet-gum stickwork sculpture created by Patrick Dougherty, a stunning display of environmental art.

I'll find inspiration in Brevard, in Kyle Lusk's towering steel banjo in front of the United Methodist church, and in the unexpected portrait of a sunglasses-wearing Beethoven in the alley off Main Street.

I'll find beauty on familiar buildings, the ones with a story and a history, in the artwork of Hickory native Hunter Speagle, with his larger-than-life mural on the side of Lindy's Furniture, telling the story of the "Miracle of Hickory," and in the work of Napolean Hill, whose bold images on the sides of buildings in Warren, Halifax, and Northampton counties bring to light the history of agriculture and industry in eastern North Carolina. Amid the uniform landscape out here, Hill's murals burst with color and light and energy, and isn't this what art is meant to do? To kindle a memory, to stir a heart, to persuade and provoke and surprise and mourn and delight. To pull light from the shadows. To inspire hope.

Always and eternal, art fulfills its promise, ready and waiting for us to find our spot in the sunshine and enjoy the view. **OS**

Sunshine Daydream

We called it "laying out," not tanning or sunbathing, and it required the following:

1. A reclining lawn chair, the kind with plastic striping stretched across the aluminum frame. Mine was buttercup yellow, from Roses, and, during summers in the 1980s, I put that thing to use every day.

2. Suntan oil, and yes, that's *oil* not lotion or, heaven help, sunscreen, although if you had to have some sort of protection, no more than SPF 4. Did we heed the warnings of the wise who cautioned us against burning, against damaging our skin? We did not. My neighbor's mother had a foldable sun reflector that she held under her chin. My own mother remembers slathering Crisco on her skin at the beach. My friends and I believed the ads in *Seventeen* and *Glamour* magazines, the ones that told us we needed a tan, a "savage" tan, a St. Tropez Tan, a Banana Boat tan, a Panama Jack tan, and as soon as school was out for the summer, an entire aisle of Eckerd Drug in the mall was given over to rows and rows of those bronze bottles: Hawaiian Tropic with its embossed gold label, sporty Sea & Ski, fancy Bain de Soleil. I was loyal to Coppertone, its bottle imprinted with graphic stripes in orange and yellow, a perpetual sun rising above the horizon.

3. A boom box or a Walkman, our ears ensconced in orange foam headphones, and a shoebox full of cassette tapes.

4. And, of course, you needed the sun.

Oh, how we needed the sun. After nine months cooped up in classrooms, in front of dingy chalkboards; after a long winter; after a rainy spring, we emerged from indoors to turn our faces toward the light, to soak up summer the best way we knew how. Outside.

My dad mowed the lawn without his shirt on. As a teenager, I was mortified by this, but I understood that he, too, wanted to feel the warmth of sunshine on his shoulders, didn't mind if his back was reddened at the end of the day, evidence of an afternoon well spent.

We believed in the curative powers of sunshine. We carried our damp laundry out to hang on the line. We lugged potted ferns to their summer home on the porch. We removed the curtains from the windows to better let the light in. We ate our lunches outside, sitting in webbed chairs in our backyards, tomato sandwiches on paper plates balanced on our knees. We planned our picnics and family reunions, all to be held outdoors, beneath a cloudless summer sky.

And at night, we still craved the light, the brilliance of stars, the glow of fireflies, the beam of floodlights in the outfield at an evening baseball game, the dazzle of sparklers and big, booming flashes of fireworks that pushed the darkness away for a moment, at least, our summers seared in memory, permanently radiant and golden.

After a long winter, after a rainy spring, we emerged to turn our faces toward the light.

Family Trees

Here I was in the front yard of the house at near-dark, plucking leaves from low-hanging branches and shoving them by the fistful into a canvas tote to bring inside and dump out across the dining room table. *Don't wait 'til the last minute to start this project*, the teacher had admonished, and yet that's exactly what I'd done, putting off my seventh-grade science assignment, a leaf identification project, until, well, now, a few days before it was due.

We were required to collect leaves from a dozen or so trees around Randolph County over the course of a month and mount them in a three-ring binder. Identify each leaf by its common name, scientific name, whether it came from a deciduous or a coniferous tree, and give a description of each.

Thanks to my procrastination, I can't imagine I got a very good grade on the project, and although it's been almost 40 years, I regret not putting in more time and effort and thought. If I could go back and gather again, what would I collect from the ground, from the branches? What would I put in that three-ring binder?

For the first page, I'd surely clip the glossy-green leaves from the massive

magnolia tree, *Magnolia grandiflora*, that stood up the hill from my grandmother's house. In the heat of summer, she and I walked up to the tree so that she could snip a few stems for a vase. It wasn't even our tree — it belonged to the City of Asheboro and was technically on the grounds of the county courthouse — but in the '60s, she worked in the register of deeds department there, and she still knew folks who assured her with a wink that it'd be just fine if she pruned up that tree a little. To this day, I can't walk past a magnolia without pressing my nose to the blossoms, an instant olfactory transport to my grandmother's house, so filled with ambrosial sweetness.

To this day, I can't walk past a magnolia without pressing my nose to the blossoms.

I'd certainly seek out the pointed leaves of the eastern black walnut, *Juglans nigra*, that was spread out all over the property at my great-uncle's farm in Ramseur, where we gathered for family reunions, a rare chance to visit with cousins who tromped with me beneath those trees, entertaining ourselves by trying to crush, flatten, or somehow pulverize the impenetrable husks of those nuts.

I'd look for the curved leaves of the pecan tree, *Carya illinoinensis*, a reminder of the countless pies I've eaten, the nuts scooped from backyards and delivered in baskets by good neighbors.

And I'd definitely search for oaks. Not the willow oaks or pin oaks or red oaks, but the kind that filled my parents' property, the white oaks, *Quercus alba*, their roots buried deep in the clay soil, their leaves in autumn burnished to shades of brown and maroon.

Oh, there were so many acorns! A substratum of woody shells underfoot, beneath the layer of leaves that my parents spent hours raking, heaping on a tarp, dragging to the ditches. I remember the smell of those smoldering leaves, early evening trails of smoke wafting from the piles set aflame. For some, autumn is the smell of pumpkin spice; for me, it's leaf smoke, all musk and incense, a burnt offering to a new season, a blessing for the gifts of the earth, for all generations. **OS**

Life Before Air Conditioning

Growing up, a sweltering summer day spent on the front porch with Grandma was as sweet as iced tea.

These days, I'm cold all the time — at work, in movie theaters, in restaurants — blasted by unrelenting, arctic air-conditioning. I carry a sweater with me everywhere, even on the hottest mid-90 degree days. But I can remember how, not long ago, when the last month of summer would settle on us, heavy with its humidity and heat, we did what we could to stay cool.

My grandmother got the laundry out to the clothesline early, carrying the basket of just-washed linens and cotton dish towels and nightgowns to the backyard, and I helped her, cradling those clothes in my arms for as long as I could before pinning them to the line, savoring the coolness of damp fabric.

We fried okra for lunch and sliced tomatoes and ate cucumbers, the six-inch pickling kind, soaked in salt and vinegar, so cold and light and refreshing.

The temperature reading on top of Randolph Savings and Loan in downtown Asheboro told us how hot it was, as if we didn't already know from the grass in the yard, gone stiff like straw; as if we didn't already know from our sunburned skin flaking off our shoulders like a papery onion.

My grandmother and I spent our afternoons on her front porch, hoping to pick up a little bit of a breeze on the swing. She kept our glasses of tea filled with ice, and we pressed those sweating glasses to our wrists, a trick she taught me — it works! — and, thinking about it now, I can easily feel the shock of cold traveling through my body, carried along on the blood vessels.

My grandmother collected folding fans, the accordion kind printed with exotic scenes. My favorite was made of silk and lace, and she let me play with it often, folding and unfolding with a flick of my wrist, covering my face like a 10-year-old Southern geisha. For cooling, though, nothing beat her cardboard fan advertising the Blue Cross

We'd swing on the porch, and wrung out by the heat and lulled by the rhythm, I'd drift off to sleep.

Blue Shield insurance my grandfather sold. It had a wooden handle like a tongue depressor, and as we'd swing on the porch, my grandmother would get that fan going, and before long, wrung out by the heat and lulled by the rhythm of her arm moving back and forth, I'd slump beside her and drift off to sleep.

In the late '70s, my grandparents installed a window unit, a Frigidaire with wood-grain panels, in the kitchen. On its maximum setting, that thing blew such icy air that my teeth throbbed when I stood next to it. In the hottest part of the day, we'd close the windows, which meant that the sheers in the living room no longer swayed when an afternoon shower came up. And I hate to say it, but we stopped sitting on the porch as much and stayed indoors instead, in front of the television, walled off from the sweltering heat outside, yes, but also from the perfumed fragrance of creamy magnolias in the evening; from the flicker of lightning bugs hovering above the grass; from the trill of tree crickets and katydids; from the goodnight tuba call of an occasional bullfrog.

I'm grateful for modern conveniences that have given us relief and comfort, but sometimes I wonder if we gave up something in exchange — permission to enjoy August's dormancy, to let the cycle of the summer still us and give us pause. **Os**

For the Win

He trekked to Kenan Stadium in the fall for football and caught matinees at The Varsity in the winter and bought Billie Holiday's *Lady Sings the Blues* and Harry Belafonte's *Calypso* from Kemp's. He picked up his starched button-downs from Tar Heel Cleaners on Franklin and took dates to Dairyland for the Royal Banana Split, 39 cents, and bought potatoes and potted meat from Fowler's Food Store. At the close of basketball season on March 1, 1957, he cheered from the stands at Duke Indoor Stadium as his beloved Tar Heels capped an undefeated season, led by "big Len," Lennie Rosenbluth, and on that day in his sophomore year, my dad became a fan for life.

For the next 58 years, he rarely missed watching a game, and not just Carolina basketball, either. He got a kick out of Coach K's Cameron Crazies, loved watching Spud Webb dunk for NC State and Muggsy Bogues dart down the court for the Demon Deacons.

Truth be told, my dad was a fan of all sports; he respected the drive and passion of players, admired their commitment to excellence, appreciated the tension of competition. As a spectator, he felt the exhilaration of a win and the despair of a loss. I can still hear his hushed whispers of "get in the hole" for Jack or Fuzzy or Tiger. He loved Chris and Steffi and Martina, and I remember him handing me his old wooden Bancroft racket when I said I wanted to learn how to play the game myself and spent the spring knocking tennis balls against the side of the house.

He followed track and field; his health — he had a weakened heart from a bout of rheumatic fever as a child — had prohibited him from playing sports, but he'd managed the track team at Carolina and later, when I was a kid, he listened to all

of the American Legion Post 45 baseball games on WKXR-AM 1260 in Asheboro.

After the NC Sports Hall of Fame announced its 2020 inductees, I got the urge to spend a day at the gallery, on the third floor of the North Carolina Museum of History in Raleigh. If you haven't been, here's what you'll see: Richard Petty's stock car gleaming in that signature Petty Blue; Enos Slaughter's baseball bat; an exhibit devoted to Appalachian State University's jaw-dropping 2007 football win over the University of Michigan; banners and pennants honoring more than 400 players and coaches. And at the end of the hall devoted to basketball, you'll see a television replaying games.

Watching it again, I understand that this is why games are played, and why we watch.

Watch. There's UNC defeating Georgetown in the 1982 NCAA Final Four, No. 23 shining like a superstar; there's Wake Forest winning the ACC in 1961 and 1962. And then there's the 1983 NCAA game between NC State and the University of Houston, and suddenly, I'm no longer in the museum, but back in the den with my dad, my Monday night homework pushed aside, the two of us riveted to the screen, Lorenzo Charles making his winning dunk, two seconds before the buzzer, and there's the coach, Jim Valvano, bouncing across the court, overcome with excitement, jumping, twisting, and my dad, the forever Carolina fan, jumps up, too, electrified, elated. Watching it again, I understand that this is why games are played, and why we watch, and how, in these unforgettable moments replayed so many years later, we can feel so alive. **OS**

A View From the Table

From my seat at the Thanksgiving table — a card table set up in the living room for us kids and covered with a harvest gold, paper tablecloth — I can see my grandmother's Pilgrim salt-and-pepper shakers, a once-a-year switch from her Depression-glass Anchor Hocking ones, on the kitchen table, where the food is laid out, buffet-style. I can see the turkey, a 24-pound whopper, perfectly cooked and sliced with her electric knife on the sterling silver platter that she let me polish with Wright's silver cream. I see two sheet pans full of dressing, cut into squares. Bowls piled with mashed potatoes, squash casserole, green beans. There's a pottery stoneware pitcher of sweet tea — if I look at the bottom, I know I'll see a "Jugtown" stamp — and I can see the electric percolator set up on the counter beside the sink; the adults refill their coffee cups all day. There are pies — pumpkin, sweet potato, chocolate chess — on the counter, too, next to a thawing container of Cool Whip, a food that didn't even exist 10 years ago, but that my grandfather is so taken with, he eats it by the spoonful.

My younger cousins sit at the table with me, and we watch the parades on television while we eat, but with the volume off so that we can make out the conversation in the dining room. I hear my mom and dad laughing, the occasional flick of a cigarette lighter. I hear a chair scoot back; my grandmother's long beads click against the edge of the table as she gets up to flip the record — *Mantovani's Golden Hits* — on the sideboard turntable. I hear my uncles chattering about politics, my grandfather talking about golf. I catch the names Jimmy Carter and Jack Nicklaus.

From my seat at the Thanksgiving table, years later, after my grandfather died and my grandmother moved from her house to a retirement apartment owned by Asheboro Friends Church, I can see the paper turkey centerpiece from the Hallmark shop that just opened in the newly built Randolph Mall, where, now that I have my driver's license, I hang out on weekends. I can see the turkey, a 12-pounder, in its roasting pan; my grandmother keeps

My mom and I raise our glasses and toast to all the memories, grateful that we've made so many.

her silver boxed up and in storage now. We all fit around one table, and the conversation drifts to politics and sports. I catch the names Ronald Reagan and Michael Jordan at UNC.

From my seat at the Thanksgiving table — at my mother's house now — I can see a white pillar candle, lit and burning bright. I can see the turkey — just a breast, three pounds — waiting for us on the counter in the kitchen, along with a small pan of dressing, my grandmother's recipe. And instead of sweet tea, my mom and I share a bottle of wine.

We don't talk about politics or sports, although we do turn on a football game. We like hearing the sounds of a crowd in the background, how the rising voices of celebration on TV fill in the empty spaces, and although my grandmother would never have had any of the wine, my mom and I raise our glasses and toast to all the memories, grateful that we've made so many. And at some point in the afternoon, my mom will knock on her neighbors' doors or make a few phone calls to the people for whom Thanksgiving has become so sparse, and I'll hear her say, "Come join us, honey. We've got plenty."

That, we do.

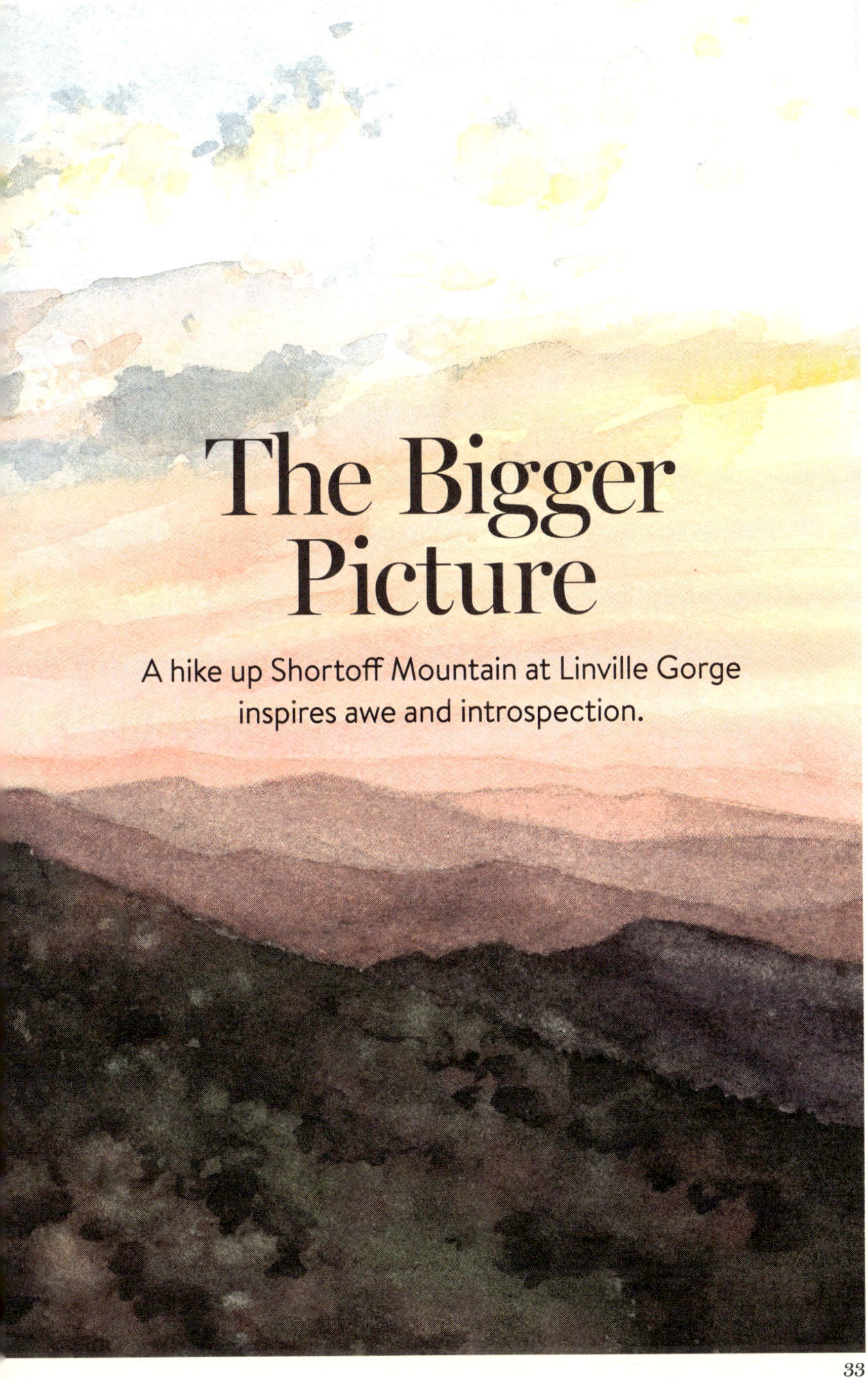

The Bigger Picture

A hike up Shortoff Mountain at Linville Gorge inspires awe and introspection.

At the Burke County Visitors Center in Morganton, Ed Phillips, who oversees tourism in this area, will ask you what kind of car you're in.

You want to get to that landmark you saw from the highway, Table Rock, overlooking Linville Gorge. You want to drive, or hike, to the summit of Hawksbill, to Wiseman's View, to Sitting Bear Mountain. There are roads, Ed will assure you, but some are unpaved and rough enough that you need a high-clearance vehicle. There are trails, Ed will say, but some are rocky and strenuous. Are you wearing good hiking shoes? Can you make the steep climb? We don't want you getting lost or, worse, hurt. Ed will say that to you, too.

To say that Linville Gorge is one of the most breathtakingly beautiful places in this state is an understatement. It's jaw-droppingly beautiful, in part because of its wildness, a primordial landscape that, in many places, looks untouched for eons. It's vast and rugged, and, yes, with those conditions also comes potential for danger, which is why Ed is careful to ask the right questions.

It was deemed a wilderness area in 1951 and received its official recognition in 1964, when President Johnson signed the Wilderness Act into law. Because of that designation, which was intended to minimize human interference, trails aren't marked clearly; roads aren't allowed; you can't even bring a chainsaw in to cut fallen trees — local volunteer crews work with hand tools to keep trails as accessible as possible. This is an area, the Wilderness Act asserts, "where earth and its community of life are untrammeled by man, where man himself is a visitor who does not remain."

But that doesn't mean visitors aren't welcome, and on my first trip to the gorge, I stopped in to ask Ed a few questions, threw on a backpack — do you have water? Ed will ask you that, too — and set off to hike four miles up Shortoff Mountain.

A half-mile into the climb, Lake

Linville Gorge is jaw-droppingly beautiful, in part because of its wildness.

James comes into view. Trek higher and you'll start watching for peregrine falcons and hawks that might soar overhead; you'll find yourself stopping at every rock overlook to peer gingerly over the edge.

What is it about the view from such an elevation that makes you look down?

Keep climbing and you'll see the scrubby Table Mountain pines that seed during wildfires; flip over rocks and you might find salamanders, fishing spiders, delicate jack-in-the-pulpits. Higher still, and a crop of British soldiers — tiny lichen plants with brilliant red caps — come into view, their color a miniature blaze of drama amid a landscape already overwhelming in its beauty; everywhere the terrain an awe-inspiring spectacle.

At the top, where wisps of clouds cloak the rounded shoulders of these mountains, where the canyon walls rise high above the sliver of the Linville River below, you stop to rest.

What is it about the view from such an elevation that makes you look up?

And here, in the silence, another question comes: What do you think of it all? What do you think of this glorious landscape, of this geologic wonder? What do you think of this most magnificent creation, preserved and protected? And you hear your whispered answer: Wow.

And thank you. **OS**

Christmas in Toyland

I can't forget the big gifts, the ones that made it from my wish list to under the tree, the ones that made me buzz with excitement on Christmas morning: Barbie's three-story town house with its fancy scrollwork elevator that ascended with a drawstring; the Sit 'N Spin on which I twirled for hours on the kitchen floor; the Schwinn Fair Lady with its gleaming whitewall tires; the Baby Alive doll with its packets of food mix and extra set of diapers.

Not yet fully awake, my mom and dad sat together on the couch, drinking coffee and quietly exchanging the gifts they'd gotten each other. Big gifts make an impression, but it's the smaller ones I remember now — the leather moccasin slippers my mom gave my dad every year to replace the ones with holes worn through the soles; the jar of hand cream he gave her to soothe her winter-chapped hands.

Before the living room floor became covered with shreds of wrapping paper, my dad steered my mom and me toward our Christmas stockings, the ones he filled himself: a bottle of Estée Lauder

All these years later, it hits me as a surprise, and those childhood joys come right back. The gift of memory.

Youth-Dew and Lady Gillette razors for her, the same every year, but tucked into mine were simple surprises, old-timey toys I hadn't even known to wish for.

Here lived the nonelectric toys, the ones that didn't need batteries, the ones without cords to plug in or parts to connect. An egg of Silly Putty, a Blues Band harmonica, a plastic spud gun. With each toy, my dad leaned in, showing me how to press the putty onto a newspaper comic strip and stretch out Snuffy Smith's face; how to blow into the numbered holes of the harmonica; how to spear a potato in just the right way to make a pellet. Together, we launched Arrowcopters across the room with rubber bands. I'd spend half an afternoon trying to get my Duncan Imperial yo-yo to "walk the dog" — watch me, Dad, watch me!

As a teenager, when the big gifts were no longer toys but sweaters or cassette tapes, my dad still filled my stocking with a tin of jacks or a deck of cards, offering to spend an afternoon showing me how to play solitaire. In my 20s, when the big gifts were no longer toys but cash to help with rent, I'd find, shoved into the toe, multicolored Pez dispensers, a wooden Jacob's ladder, a metal Slinky. He kept it going, every year, into my 30s, into my 40s, for as long as he could.

Of course, I outgrew the Speak & Spell, the Lite-Brite, the Easy-Bake Oven. The Atari 2600 video game console is long gone, as is the Snoopy Sno-Cone Machine, the Casio digital watch. But somehow, those simple toys inside my stocking outlasted everything else. Every now and then, all these years later, I'll come across something tucked away in a shoebox, at the back of a desk drawer, and it hits me as a surprise every time, the discovery of one of these small stocking stuffers that I never parted with — a rubber Super Ball, a wooden triangle peg game, an old yo-yo. I loop the string around my finger and flick my wrist, dropping the spool the way my dad taught me — watch me, Dad, watch me — and those childhood joys come right back. The gift of memory. The string pulls and the yo-yo spins and hovers above the ground before it snaps back toward my palm. I catch it and hold on for just a second before I release it again. **Os**

Winter Outlook

You can see the face, that recognizable face — the forehead, the nose, the jutting chin of the Old Man, the reclining profile that is Grandfather Mountain — from the dining room of Grandview Restaurant in Banner Elk, just beyond your plate of biscuits and white gravy, beyond your bacon and eggs and hash browns.

You can see it from the ninth fairway at Hound Ears Club golf course, that familiar rock face rising nearly 6,000 feet above the earth, its gaze toward the heavens, anchored in place as it has been for a billion years.

You can see it from NC Highway 105 in Foscoe; in the winter, the profile is veiled in snow, its beard dappled white, yet the semblance is always there, the comfort of an age-old, immemorial landscape.

For four days in the fall, I saw the profile of Grandfather Mountain every morning from the deck of a vacation house in Boone, having been lucky to find a spot with such an extraordinary view. I drank my morning coffee and watched the clouds skim across the top of the mountain, watched a midday rain shower settle over the valley, watched shafts of afternoon sunlight bathe the trees in a glorious shimmer.

How many places in North Carolina can claim views like this? A dozen? A hundred?

I think of sunrise over Old Lighthouse Beach in Buxton, a sight that'll hold you spellbound, and the sweeping view from the gallery of the Cape Hatteras Lighthouse. It'll leave

you breathless, and not just from climbing the 257 steps, but also from that expansive vista of treetops leading to the open sea, a beauty to behold.

I think of the views closer to home, the ones that take me back to the landscapes I knew. I can see my grandmother looking out over her flower garden, dormant in winter but readying for blooms of early crocus. I can see my dad looking out the windows of our old house in Randolph County, the gently sloping Uwharries in the distance, far less elevation than the Blue Ridge, but just as enduring.

I think of the views closer to home. Views don't have to be dramatic to be memorable.

When my parents moved to a townhouse in Greensboro, away from views they'd known for so many years, my dad still found a place by the window. He worked his crossword puzzle every morning and watched for the birds, chickadees and northern cardinals, to gather at his feeders. He watched for deer that appeared in the early evening; he excitedly called for my mom when he saw the first flakes of snow drifting from the sky. Views don't have to be dramatic to be memorable.

Now, from my own window on quiet winter evenings, with the tree canopy sparse and the horizon unobscured, I wait for my favorite view, a moonrise, luminous in a cloudless sky. I can make out the shadows on the surface, the ones that give the illusion of a face, the fabled man in the moon — the Old Man — eternal in its place in the sky. And I can imagine that it's looking back at me, reflecting light, full of hope, shining and so bright. OS

You Make My Heart Sing

A symphony of soothing birdsong is a balm for the soul.

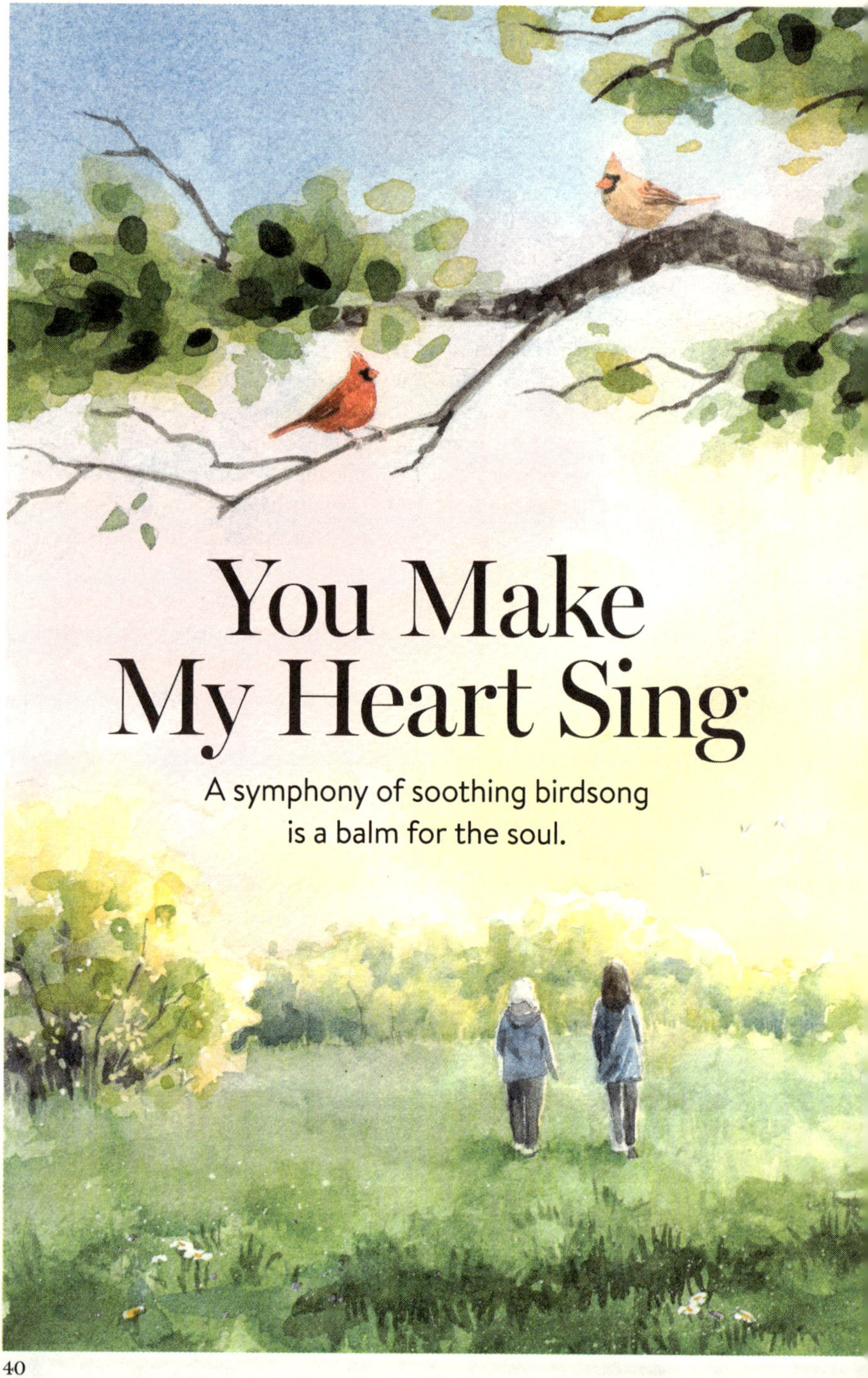

It's the first sound I hear in the morning, before the coffee maker clicks on and steam spatters against the hot burner, before a squirrel patters across the roof: the sharp, high, clear-whistled voice of an American robin, perched somewhere outside my window, just before sunrise. He's there every day, his sweet song rising with the first light, his lilt nudging me awake, his bright, fluty notes lifting my heart.

These tiny birds fill the morning with a symphony of sound, a full choral concert. Nature's ode to joy.

By the time I'm outside for my morning walk, the sky has lightened, and the robins have been joined by wrens, Carolina chickadees, and white-throated sparrows, these tiny birds trilling with their whole hearts and filling the morning with a symphony of sound, a full choral concert. Nature's ode to joy.

I've heard these songs all my life, familiar notes that never seem to change. On spring weekends, before my grandmother called me in for lunch, uprooting me from the hammock in her backyard, I'd listen to the bluebirds that were drawn to her garden for the flowering dogwood trees and for the birdbaths that she always kept filled. On quiet summer evenings, just before dusk, we'd catch the soothing coo of a mourning dove.

In later years, when I'd help her walk to Asheboro Friends Meetings for the Sunday service, we'd stop often so that she could catch her breath. Holding onto my shoulder for steadiness, she'd look up, hopeful, her eyes scanning the treetops, the skies. Or maybe beyond; I was never sure. Then we'd hear it — the *pew-pew* of a Northern cardinal perched on a branch of the church's magnolia tree. He sang every Sunday, as if he'd been waiting there for an audience.

My grandmother loved hymns, and it's only now, when I hear the songs of her beloved birds, that I recall the lines she loved best: *Each little flower that opens/Each little bird that sings*, from "All Things Bright and Beautiful." And this one: *When through the woods and forest glades I wander/And heard the birds sing sweetly in the trees*, from "How Great Thou Art."

Then sings my soul, indeed.

I think of the birds that converged on my parents' backyard: goldfinches and red-bellied woodpeckers and brown-headed nuthatches, attracted to the feeders full of sunflower seeds, millet, and peanuts; enticed by the nesting houses and roosting boxes that my dad built. I remember how he stood at the kitchen window in the mornings, stirring sugar into his coffee and watching a flock of birds flitting outside, proud to have created such a safe and hospitable place, such a welcoming environment.

No matter where I go in North Carolina — a walk through a longleaf forest in Southern Pines or a rose garden in Wilson; a trek along a trail at Grandfather Mountain or a visit to Fort Fisher — the birds are always there, too, singing, calling, cooing, peeping, chirping, their voices perennial, perpetual, a ceaseless reminder that I, too, am home. **OS**

Finding a Calling

Our telephone, a beige Western Electric with a rotary dial, held a place of honor in our old house in Asheboro: perched in a built-in phone nook in the hallway. It was hardwired into the wall, and, persuaded by that Bell Systems TV commercial to "reach out; reach out and touch someone," I'd camp out in the hall after supper and call someone from school.

I had my own personal address book, pink vinyl with a Holly Hobbie illustration on the cover. My grandmother had a metal, flip-style directory with a slide that corresponded to the alphabet and a button that popped the cover open to the last name. I loved that thing. She used it for phone numbers, but also recorded details like birthdays and anniversaries in it. In our house, a shelf beneath the phone held the city phone book. Back then, aside from the Bible and maybe a set of World Book Encyclopedias, I can't think of another book that was in every household besides a telephone directory.

I called Asheboro's Time-and-Temperature line. I called the library's Dial-A-Story. When we moved to our new home near Farmer, I was allowed to pick out my own phone for my room. I chose a canary-yellow Trimline with push buttons. I stayed on the phone so much that I could even tap out songs. (In case you wondered, 1-1-2-1-#-6 plays "Happy Birthday.")

The older I got, the more the phone became a lifeline. It was the first thing I packed when I went off to college, calls from friends a balm during the coldest winter at Appalachian State. Maybe you know that when I was hired at this magazine 25 years ago, my first job was to answer the telephone.

Eventually, time and technology moved forward, and my phone usage diminished. I abandoned a landline for a cell phone years ago, voice communication largely replaced by emails and texts.

Recently, I got a voice mail, a short, 30-second message from a man named James McGee in Asheville. He called simply to say that he was enjoying the magazine. He didn't ask for a return call, but I made one anyway.

We talked for nearly 45 minutes, and

the veneer of strangers fell away as he told me about growing up in the "Land of the Sky," the place that he loved most until he discovered the "Southern Part of Heaven" in 1948. Of course, I knew what he meant, having heard that same endearment from my dad, and I laughed, and Mr. McGee kept the stories going as I listened, riveted. He recounted drives from Chapel Hill to Greensboro in his black Plymouth for dances at "the WC," and he didn't say, but I could imagine the strains of Art Mooney looking over a four-leaf clover. He talked of stopping at Brady's on Durham Road for fried chicken, and finishing pharmacy school at UNC and moving back to Asheville and buying Kenilworth Drug Store and marrying his sweetheart, Margo, a schoolteacher, 69 years ago on December 28, the same day as her birthday so that, as she told him, "You'll never forget our anniversary." He told me that Margo died two years ago and I heard the catch in his voice, over the phone, through the miles, across the radio waves, how much he misses her.

All week, I've been replaying that conversation with Mr. McGee and how much I enjoyed it, an unexpected connection that reminded me of the gift of voices, the ones we all need, the ones that ease us through our times of silence. **OS**

The conversation was an unexpected connection that reminded me of the gift of voices.

Heart, Shaped

If I'm treating myself, I'm going for the classic chocolate caramel bonbons from French Broad Chocolate Lounge, packaged in a little blue box, North Carolina's version of Tiffany blue; or maybe I'm going for the triple chocolate truffle from Chocolate Fetish in Asheville, with its three layers of opulence. If I'm in Raleigh, it's definitely the gold-tinged honey caramel bonbons from the chocolate counter at Videri Chocolate Factory or the dark chocolate sea salt bar from Escazu. My first experience with that last one came in Beaufort more than a decade ago, when one of North Carolina's first chocolate pioneers, Hallot Parson, had just started producing small-batch candy from his little apartment above Cru Wine Bar.

But on one day each year, February 14 — Valentine's Day — I look forward to something else: my heart-shaped, wrapped-in-red-cellophane box of assorted chocolates from, yes, Russell Stover, a tradition started by my dad when I was 6 years old, and now taken over by my mother, as neither of us can imagine a Valentine's Day without it.

In the 1950s, after my dad left school at UNC, he lived for a while in Kansas City, Missouri, and along with an affinity for (and insistence on) pronouncing the state name "Missour-uh," he came back home with a love for the local chocolate sold at the Russell Stover candies store. He thought that it was, quite simply, the best, and in those years, way before independent, hand-crafted, artisanal chocolate began springing up all over North Carolina, before Dillsboro Chocolate Factory started making their pecan-and-caramel turtles, before Black Mountain Chocolate produced their cocoa nibs and peppermint bark, before Bar Cocoa in Charlotte ever dreamed of artistically swirled, ganache-filled candy, I thought so, too.

Although I was a child, I somehow understood its impermanence.

My dad, despite being tall and thin, had an undeniable sweet tooth, but only for chocolate. He kept a bowl of Hershey's Kisses within reach on the coffee table in the den, unwrapping and popping them in his mouth during ACC basketball games on TV. He stashed Tootsie Rolls in the glove compartment of his truck, and picked up boxes of Brach's Chocolate Cherry Cordials at Christmas to fill my mom's and my stockings. He loved milk chocolate Mallo Cups and Kit Kats, miniature Special Darks and Krackels, Milk Duds and Snickers and Raisinets and Creme Drops, and the candy drawer in our kitchen stayed full year-round.

That Russell Stover box, though, was a rarity, something that appeared only once during the entire year, and although I was a child, I somehow understood its impermanence. Only a dozen pieces of candy came in the box, and I was careful to dole out just a piece or two a day, to make them last as long as possible. I ate the cream-filled ones first, then the caramels, and, finally, the single chocolate coconut cluster, the one my dad called a Ting-A-Ling, because that's what the Russell Stover store called it. There was only ever one of those chocolate clusters in the box, and maybe that's why it was the best.

And every time, when I ate that one, I'd hold it up to my dad to show him, an unspoken "that's it, until next year" between us. He'd sling his arm around my shoulder and give me a squeeze — "Good, isn't it?" he'd say — and I'd nod, grateful for a box filled with chocolate and happy for a heart filled with love. **O&S**

Open Windows

In the summertime,
North Carolina's beaches have a tidal pull.

Feels like the beach was my thought on a summer-like day in Greensboro — temperature pushing past 80 with a soft wind blowing — so I threw open all the windows in my house. Cross breeze cutting through, balmy air, ceiling fan whirring, an occasional bumblebee gently bumping the window screen, and for an afternoon, at least, I could *imagine* being at the beach, back at places so familiar and friendly.

For a moment, I'm at the Blockade Runner Resort in Wrightsville Beach, on a balcony overlooking a manicured courtyard popping with blooming hibiscus and tropical birds-of-paradise; arching pindo palms with their pineapple-y bases; canna lilies blazing orange and red, echoing the colors of the maritime signal flags flapping from the boardwalk.

For a moment, I'm kicking back in a swinging rattan chair at the Atlantis Lodge in Pine Knoll Shores, bare feet brushing the weathered gray deck, a cup of coffee in hand, just brewed in the room's kitchenette. The Atlantis is dog-friendly, and I love seeing the guests' pets, tails lazily thumping in the sun, puppies with their cold noses, with their warm hearts, nudging their owners for a Frisbee throw, for a run on the beach, for a chance to dig in the sand.

I can't wait for the chance to unlatch the door to my own screened porch overlooking the dunes of the Outer Banks at the Sanderling Resort in Duck; the hotel even stocks rooms with a complimentary s'mores kit to use around a firepit that's lit at sundown.

I'm remembering the Golden Sands motel in Carolina Beach, the rooms just a few steps from the Ocean Grill & Tiki Bar. Got a bar stool outside on the pier beneath a string of party lights, a pail of Topsail oysters, and a frosty can of Fullsteam beer, Humidity Pale Ale.

When it's time, I'll point my car east. I'll roll down the windows and drive until I smell salt.

And just as the sun starts to drop a little lower, a band — The Shoaldiggers with their swampgrass sound, Da Howlies strumming Hawaiian music — cranks up and the pier bounces, and everyone whoops and hollers and dances in the open air.

There's the Main Street Inn in Topsail Beach, a compact but nearly perfect boutique hotel, where I sat for hours on a Friday night in a slatted rocker and swayed to the music drifting over from Patio Playground directly across the street, my own personal concert from the '60s, with Marvin Gaye and Aretha Franklin and The Beach Boys crooning "Barbara Ann" and "Surfer Girl," a soft-pedaling summer soundtrack that dropped my shoulders and soothed my spirit. A hand-lettered chalkboard sign propped in front of Patio Playground Putt-Putt read "Be Cool, Be Kind, Be Nice, Be Happy," and, back in that moment, with a Technicolor sunset widening over the Banks Channel behind the inn, it was hard to imagine any emotion other than happiness.

When it's time, I'll point my car east. I'll roll down the windows and drive until I smell salt, until I see the loblollies change over to longleafs, until I hear the lap of water beneath the Alligator River Bridge, and I'll welcome my coastal reunion. **OS**

The Special Sauce

You might think they're all the same — hamburgers — as common on any North Carolina menu as a barbecue sandwich, as sweet tea, as a fizzy fountain Pepsi. Nothing special, you might think: a plain bun, softened by the heat of a steamer; a patty smashed on a flat-top with melting American cheese. Lettuce, tomato, mayonnaise. Chili, slaw, and mustard.

Have I had a hamburger in all 100 counties? Close, I'd say; my first one ever at 5 or 6 years old, in Asheboro, of course, my hometown. On Saturdays, my grandmother and I would walk from her house across from the library, where we'd spent our morning, to Little Castle on Sunset Avenue, a small restaurant with a few booths against the wall and a calendar hanging behind the counter, its paper bronzed with grease splatters from the open grill.

Later, there was Ray's Kingburger, where we'd drive after a day at the swimming pool, the upswept, triangle-shaped peak of Ray's roof rising like a steeple, a mecca for burgers.

We went to Golden Waffle for the Master Burger Plate, two patties, and Brown-Gardiner in Greensboro for a burger with an orangeade, and when I got tired of the cafeteria food during my first year at Appalachian State University and wanted nothing more than to be back home, I'd trek from my dorm on the hill down to King Street for a burger at the counter at Boone Drug. I'd ease onto one of those yellow vinyl swivel stools and listen to the patties sizzling on the grill, the spatula scraping against the flat-top, and I'd feel better.

My dad always said, "Order the burger." If they could get that right, they'd get everything right.

My dad always said, "Order the burger" in any restaurant, believing that if they could get that right, they'd get everything right. In his sandwich shop, where I'd twirl on the swivel stools and watch him flatten burgers on the griddle, he'd sometimes let me lean over the counter and press the lever on the Fresh-O-Matic

bun steamer, a gentle whoosh of warm air as comforting as a sigh.

And maybe it was because he cooked them all day, but we never had burgers at home. Ground beef was for meat loaf, for spaghetti sauce, for chili beans. At my grandmother's, we ate country-style steak and buttermilk biscuits, but she never made hamburgers, either. Those were weekend treats, food we went out for on sunlit afternoons after a day of doing nothing, which is to say, after a perfect day.

I think I've been chasing those burgers that I remember, the ones that remind me of those perfect days, all over North Carolina. I've found them at Second Street Lunch in Roanoke Rapids; at Mamie's Drive In in Laurel Hill, a double enjoyed outside on a picnic table; at Johnson's in Siler City, where the cooks pile on slabs of Velveeta; at Fat Andy's in Southport, one all the way, wrapped in tinfoil and scarfed down under a pine tree; at Miller's in Mocksville, a burger dressed with pimento cheese; at Duke's in Monroe, loaded with slaw.

Yes, you can get a burger anywhere in North Carolina. But places like these are time machines, delivering something extra special — more than lettuce, tomato, mayonnaise; chili, slaw, and mustard — that keeps us coming back. **Os**

There's No Place Like Home

Just got back from a weeklong magazine conference at Yale University in New Haven, Connecticut, which seems to be a pretty nice school. I was excited to tour a new area and, on my first day, I spent some time wandering the Old Campus. Passed the windowless building that houses the secret Skull and Bones society, and, while it was neat, I don't mind admitting to you that I puffed up with a bit of pride when I compared it to our own Gimghoul Castle in Chapel Hill, with its mysterious secret society, set among those classic Carolina pines.

I popped into the Peabody Museum of Natural History and saw their gem and mineral exhibit — really impressive, but I smiled when I realized we've got something like that, too, at the Pisgah Astronomical Research Institute near Brevard, which houses a world-class collection of gems, including one of the largest emeralds ever found on earth and some of the earliest meteorites to ever fall from space.

New Haven also claims some of the best pizza in the country, a reputation that comes from its legendary coal-fired brick ovens, so I had to try it, and sure, it was outstanding, but I couldn't help but think of one of my favorite spots, Cugino Forno Pizzeria in Greensboro — the word forno means "oven" in Italian — with their handmade, rock-bottomed ovens created from sand and stone imported from Mount Vesuvius.

He put a comforting hand on my shoulder and told me how much he'd enjoyed visiting my state.

On my second day in New Haven, my tour took an unexpected turn when I started to feel sick. I tried to stave off whatever was coming with Advil and apple juice; day three was a little worse,

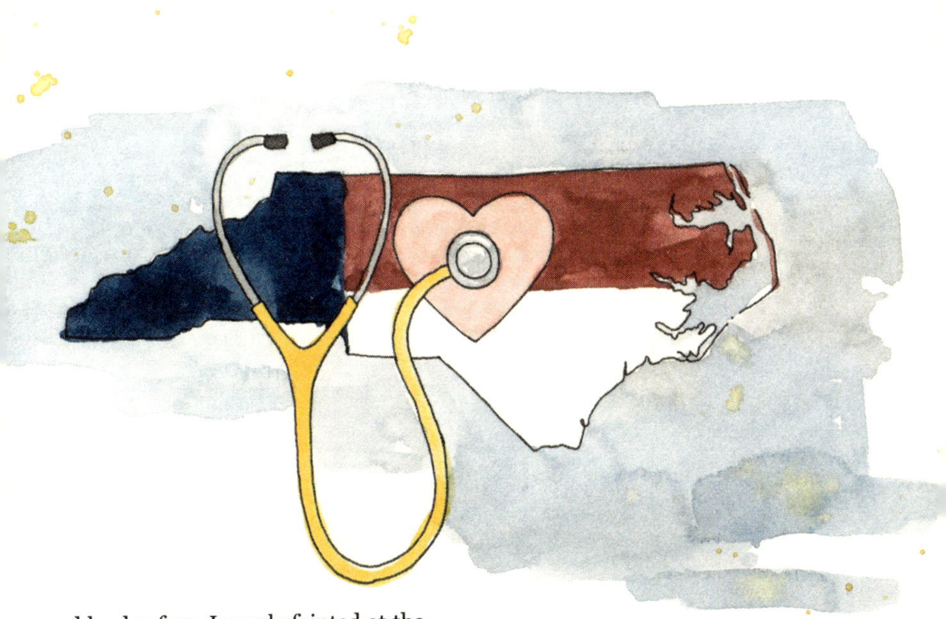

and by day four, I nearly fainted at the conference, overcome with pain in my jaw, fever, chills. I got whisked off to the Yale Health Center, where a doctor hooked me up to some wires for an electrocardiogram and, to distract me from my nervousness, asked me where I was visiting from.

North Carolina, I told him. His face lit up. One of his best vacations was spent at the Outer Banks, he said, and while we talked about surfing at Nags Head and bicycling along NC Highway 12, my blood pressure, sky-high when I came in, dropped to normal.

He sent me on to the ER, and as I was checking in, an orderly heard my Southern accent and came over to ask where I lived. Greensboro, I said, and he whooped — his best friend graduated from A&T University before going on to Wake Forest for law school. He put a comforting hand on my shoulder and told me how much he'd enjoyed visiting my state.

I got pumped full of penicillin to fight a bacterial infection, and the doctors assured me I'd be fine. I'm home now, and well, but as I lay on a hospital bed, 600 miles from home, alone and frightened, a nurse came in and read my file. She saw me shivering and draped me in a blanket that had been warmed in a dryer. She was gentle when she extended my arm for the IV and told me that she'd spent a decade working as a nurse at Carolinas Medical Center in Charlotte. She told me how much she loved the cornbread from Mert's Heart and Soul and how she'd spend her days off in the orchid conservatory at Daniel Stowe Botanical Garden. I took a deep breath, thinking of all the places I love, too, and started to feel better. **OS**

Miles to Go

On the Blue Ridge Parkway, drivers discover that the journey *is* the destination.

On the Blue Ridge Parkway, there are only two directions you can go: north or south. Follow the walnut-colored arrows on the signposts pointing the way on a road that has not been widened, has not been rerouted, has not been altered in more than 80 years.

Those weathered signs share space, unobtrusively, on the shoulder of the road with dogwood and tulip trees, with white-blooming rosebay rhododendrons and flame azaleas; with soft pink mountain laurel and violet joe-pye weed; with crimson maples and brilliant ochre oaks. At the Air Bellows Overlook, stands of Christmas trees sweep the sloping valley below. At the Stone Mountain Overlook, the exposed granite dome, streaked in shades of cream and khaki, pops out barefaced amid the leafy hills. At the Thunder Hill Overlook, the deep pinks of a spring sunrise, the feverish oranges of an autumn sunrise, the noble purples of a winter sunrise will take your breath.

For everything the parkway has, it's what the parkway lacks that makes it so special.

On the parkway, there is fog: Clouds sink in a thermal inversion; cold air descends; a hazy veil drops over the view. On the parkway, there is wind: light fall breezes, just enough to stir the limbs of a poplar, just enough to scatter fallen leaves; occasionally, gusts of more than 100 miles per hour. On the parkway, there is snow: a dusting, a coating, a blanket.

On the parkway, there are fences, hand-built by WPA workers from American chestnut salvaged from the blight: the curving snake style, the post-and-rail construction, the crosshatched "buck" fence — rustic sculptures framing fields, meadows, pastureland.

But for everything that the parkway has — panoramic overlooks and pastoral views; picturesque stone bridges and tunnels; stubs of mile markers, blue numbers recessed into the concrete — it's what the parkway lacks that makes it so special.

On the parkway, there are no billboards or advertisements of any kind. You won't share the road with trucks, tractor trailers, or commercial vans with logos of business emblazoned on the side. There are no road signs for motels, hotels, grocery stores, convenience shops, car dealerships, boats, or banks.

There are no white lines on the parkway's edges, a deliberate design choice all those years ago to ensure that painted markings wouldn't conflict with the palette of nature.

There are no stoplights on the parkway, and yet, here on this road, we're able to find a sense of pause. An instinctive slowdown.

How lucky we are to have this road, its purpose for beauty not only fulfilled but also protected, guarded for generations, a future continuing as far into the distance as we can see. ***OS***

Scenes from a Museum

I hadn't taken a single art class in school, owing to the fact that my artistic ability is limited to doodles and stick figures. I'd never helped paint a poster for a class president or papier-mâché'd a float for homecoming, and I most certainly was not a member of the high school art club. Yet none of that stopped me from walking out of homeroom one morning and boarding the school's activity bus for a field trip that the art club was taking to the North Carolina Museum of Art in Raleigh.

At my grandmother's house, framed landscape oil paintings by her sister, my great-aunt Dorothy, hung on the walls, and at Christmas, we displayed *Norman Rockwell's Christmas Book* on the coffee table. At home, my dad had books about the photography of Ansel Adams and the architecture of Frank Lloyd Wright. But I'd never been in a place solely and wholly devoted to art. So when I heard that the art club had planned this trip, well, I saw an opportunity.

Did I mention that I was not a member of this club? Yet no one seemed to question my presence on the bus. I *may* have told the art teacher who was chaperoning that I was covering the event for the school newspaper (not true), and I had *perhaps* neglected to mention to my parents that I was planning to cut school to go on a field trip for which I did not have permission to go.

I'd never seen anything like it, and the impression has stayed with me my whole life.

I'd packed a sack lunch that morning and wrapped a cold can of Coke in tinfoil. It took two hours to get to Raleigh on the bus, and we scarfed down our bagged lunches on picnic tables before a docent came out to lead our tour.

Once inside, I was awestruck. I still remember being pulled toward the painting in the lobby, a 12-foot-wide modern work called *American Landscape with Revolutionary Heroes*: silhouettes of five figures, the founding fathers, were set against a color field

of gray and turquoise. I'd never seen anything like it, and the impression — amazement for the scale of a large work of art, admiration for the boldness of color — has stayed with me my whole life. That day, I saw works by Andrew Wyeth and Georgia O'Keeffe — on a trip out West a few years ago, I was overcome with emotion in front of Cebolla Church in New Mexico, the exact site of the O'Keeffe painting that I'd discovered back in Raleigh on that very first visit to the museum. I saw Greek and Egyptian sculptures, American landscapes, and French Impressionism, and I took it all in, transported from the views I knew in Randolph County to a broader, wider world, one that unfolded for me inside a museum on that day.

My trip wasn't without repercussions. Evidently, my unsanctioned absence had been noted, and when the bus returned to school, I was summoned to the principal's office. "We have to do *something*," the principal told me. Rules are rules, and I had broken them. My punishment was a day of in-school suspension. "But I don't think there's a need for us to mention this incident to your parents," the principal said, with a pat to my shoulder, earning my complete gratitude.

Since that day, I'm happy to say that I've been back to the NCMA numerous times — and not just there, but others, too. By my count, North Carolina has more than 600 museums, places devoted to art, and also to history and science, to agricultural life and military pursuits, to sports and transportation, an endless archive of knowledge and imagination.

Permission granted for all of us to come inside. **Os**

Christmas Continues

The recipe wasn't a secret; it was first printed on the side of the silver-and-brown Hershey's Unsweetened Cocoa container in the 1960s, back when the container was made of tin and you had to push a spoon or the edge of a butter knife up under the lip of the lid to pop it off. You could never really wipe off the dusting of cocoa powder that settled around the top of the container, and the metal lid always rusted, so maybe that's why Hershey's changed to a plastic container. But I don't have the answer for why they removed the fudge recipe.

I worry that there'll be a generation of people who'll never know what that old-fashioned, homemade fudge was like: crumbly, crackly, a melt-in-your-mouth texture like a buttermint, but with a firmness to it, too, different from anything you can buy in the store or even in a specialty fudge shop.

I knew it was officially Christmastime when my grandmother cleared off the table on her back porch to set out sheet pans full of fudge to cool before she cut them into cubed pieces. She made

pounds of this fudge at Christmastime for us to eat and to give as gifts, wrapping it up in festive tins that she bought at Eagles Five and Dime. We never had it any other time but during the holidays. Despite the minimal ingredients — no sweetened condensed milk or chocolate chips or nuts or marshmallows — my grandmother claimed that this fudge was notoriously difficult to make, finicky and exacting, and in her lifetime, she probably threw away as many batches as she'd made, due to the fudge crystallizing or not setting up properly.

If I closed my eyes, I could easily be transported back to my grandmother's kitchen.

You have to have a cold day, she insisted. No humidity. Bring cocoa, sugar, and milk to a boil. Do not stir! Make sure it passes the "soft ball" test by dropping a pinch of fudge into a bowl of cold water. Add butter and vanilla, let the mixture cool in the pot, and then beat the daylights out of it, always with a wooden spoon, until it loses its glossy sheen before turning it out onto a pan.

Eventually, after years of watching my grandmother make that candy, noticing techniques that can't be written down, my mother took up the mantle at our house, following the precise instructions, waiting for a cold day, using a wooden spoon, cooling the fudge in pans, wrapping it all up on festive plastic plates, and carrying forth a tradition that meant so much in our family. I remember the smell of rich chocolate boiling on the stove — the whole house would smell of chocolate all day — and if I closed my eyes, I could easily be transported back to my grandmother's kitchen, too, those sweet smells and sounds, the burble of chocolate in the pot, the slap of the spoon, the crinkle of wax paper, connecting the years as if no time had passed at all.

When Christmas gets closer and the temperature drops and my mom pulls out the ingredients for this year's batch, I'll be there with her, observing, watching, memorizing techniques that can't be written down. And when it's time — a transfer of the wooden spoon, a handed-down recipe, my own search for just the right plates — I'll be ready, keeping that link between then and now going. **Os**

Going Back

In Randolph County, the ever-flowing Deep River offers a glimpse of the past.

My grandmother kept her stack of photo albums on a shelf beneath the coffee table — large, leather, three-ring binders that stored our family memories, a lifetime of pictures encased beneath crinkly, yellowed sheets of cellophane.

I was drawn to the early albums, the ones that were "B.E." — before Elizabeth — the ones that held pictures of my dad as a baby in the '30s, outfitted in his delicate white dressing gown; the ones that showed my grandparents proudly leaning on the hood of their new Hudson Hornet; the ones that revealed first Christmases and good dogs long gone, faded vacations, and unexpected snowfalls.

I pored over the photos of people and places that I didn't have a clear recollection of, searching for traces of my own face in relatives I'd never met. I'd carry those albums to my grandmother, climb up in her chair, and beg her to "tell about the old days." And she would! How they kept eggs and buttermilk cold in the springhouse; how she learned to form smooth, cursive letters on a chalkboard slate at school; how she and her brothers and sisters played in the shallow water at the Coleridge Dam on the banks of the Deep River in southeastern Randolph County. She'd flip through those albums and point out the photo of the old homeplace in Ramseur, the two-story white farmhouse where my great-grandfather Walter Allen raised his eight children, she the next-to-youngest, and when she'd remind me that *her* middle name, Elizabeth, became *my* name, too, I'd tingle with delight, thrilled by the unity of kinship.

On a perfect blue-sky day a few weeks ago, I went down to the Deep River for a picnic by the water. I walked the rail trail converted from the Atlantic & Yadkin railroad bed that lies between Franklinville and Ramseur and realized that I couldn't have been more

In this place of deep roots, I felt a convergence: of then and now, of ancestry and history.

than a few miles from the gravesite of another of my great-grandfathers, Abraham Hudson, the town's postmaster 120 years ago. I followed an 80-year-old footbridge to a trail leading to Faith Rock, a steep bluestone outcrop rising 50 feet above the water, and I scrambled to the top for a view of the very same landscape my grandparents, my great-grandparents, surely knew as well.

I stood for a long time in this spot, watching the water burbling around the rocks in the river, lapping against the cliff ferns and holly, skirting the old fish weirs that are, remarkably, still anchored, constructed by Saponi and Keyauwee Indian tribes long ago and unmoved by weather or erosion or human intervention. Water, like time, moves in one direction — forward — but if we know where to look, we can glimpse its origin, its starting point.

Here, in this place of deep roots, I felt a convergence: of then and now, of ancestry and history, lifted by the bright, open sky and grounded by the rock beneath my feet. This rock of ages. And while I know it was just the murmur of water and the wind rustling the leaves in the trees, I could almost mistake the sounds for whispers, ancestral voices carrying through the air. I listened, grateful to feel so at home. Os

Paths Forward

More than the twisting spiral slide at Frazier Park; more than Eagles dime store with its glass-fronted candy case, where I could get a paper bag filled with my favorite chocolate stars; more than the giraffe and ostrich habitat at the North Carolina Zoo, the absolute greatest place I knew growing up in Asheboro was the Randolph County Public Library.

The side entrance was across the street from my grandmother's house, and she and I walked through those doors together every Saturday, the shiny waxed floors in the corridor widening out in front of us, gleaming like the path to Oz.

I'd make my way to the children's room, where the tables were kid-size and the bookshelves were low, the spines of the Dr. Seusses and the Childcraft encyclopedias, the Amelia Bedelias and the Frog and Toads all at eye level.

In here, I traveled along with Jess and Leslie as they explored the magical land of Terabithia, and with orphan Anne Shirley, who got sent to live on a farm called Green Gables. I listened as Jesse Tuck implored Winnie not to drink from the fountain of youth. I watched Charlotte spin a web and remind Wilbur that he had always been her friend. The discovery of one book led me down other paths: Henry Huggins introduced me to Ramona the Pest; a dive into the world of Narnia led me to the hobbits of Middle Earth.

Libraries do this: They open up rabbit holes; they drop bread crumbs; they blaze trails through forests.

Not all those who wander are lost.

At the circulation desk, the librarian — a tall woman with white hair named Miss Fox — had me print my name on the cards in the pockets of my books. I remember her red jacket, the towering way she stood over the desk, how her shoulders rounded as she stooped to show me a new book.

At 7 years old, I couldn't have known the path that led Charlesanna Fox to my library. That she graduated from the North Carolina College for Women — UNCG, my alma mater, too! — in the '30s, or that, during World War II, she'd been called to the Navy Library in Washington D.C., where she chose all the books for U.S. Navy ships.

Libraries open up rabbit holes; they drop bread crumbs; they blaze trails through forests.

I couldn't have known that when she was sent to Camp Lejeune in 1942 to become the first base librarian, she was the sole woman there, or that she served as the librarian at Pearl Harbor before returning to her hometown of Asheboro — my hometown, too! — to run the library for the next 30 years, where she showed young readers like me where to find new stories, how to follow new paths. Four years before she died in 2012, Miss Charlesanna Fox received the Order of the Longleaf Pine, one of only a handful of librarians in the state to receive such an honor.

I think she would've been proud to know that I learned all this through an oral history interview for the Women Veterans Historical Project, a special collection housed at the UNCG library. I'd been combing through their archives, researching a project that led me elsewhere, reacquainting me with a woman I remembered but didn't really know.

Libraries do this, too: They hold on to the stories we never want to forget, preserving them for the next discovery. **Os**

Easy Does It

Nowadays, you can get a hot dog loaded with whatever you want: pimento cheese, bacon bits, jalapeño peppers, sauerkraut, barbecue (I've seen it), ketchup (if you must). For me, though, the one and only way to eat a hot dog is all the way — mustard, chili, slaw, and onions — exactly the way my dad made them.

We always had a package of hot dogs in the refrigerator: Bryan's Juicy Jumbos that my dad bought wholesale to serve in his sandwich shop in Asheboro. At the restaurant, he grilled hot dogs on the flattop, but at home, for an easy summer lunch for just the two of us, he boiled them, two or three minutes in a saucepan. To fire up the charcoal grill would've taken way too long, and the key to a perfect hot dog, my dad believed, was its simplicity.

While our hot dogs boiled, he heated up a can of Patterson's Beef Hot Dog Chili (still made in Sanford the same way since 1942) and opened a container of Ruth's coleslaw (still made in Charlotte the same way since 1953). I didn't realize it then, but my dad was creating a tradition, repeating the same elements every time, coming back to the same ingredients, the same method of preparation, serving our lunch on paper plates with a handful of Charles Chips and a cold Coke in a glass bottle. He handed his hot dog preferences down to me, and now, having eaten half a lifetime worth of hot dogs all over North Carolina, I can confirm that the classic style — simple, easy — endures.

> **The key to a perfect hot dog, my dad believed, was its simplicity.**

Go inside The Dog House on Main Street in High Point, and you'll see. Their way is "loaded," and it's been the same since 1942, grilled on that flattop by the window. It's cash only here, always has been; no credit cards, no debit cards, no checks, and the waitress will ring you up on an antique brass cash register not quite original to the place but almost. You'll get your hot dog brought to the booth or the counter on a square of wax paper, no plate, easy to clean up when you finish. Simplicity at its best.

That same tradition holds at Yum Yum's in Greensboro, too, going on 116 years now, and at Pulliams in Winston-Salem, open since 1910. You'll find it at Dick's Hot Dog Stand in Wilson, 101 years old, and at Green's Lunch in Charlotte, close behind with its founding date of 1926, and at Zack's in Burlington and Bill's in Washington and Paul's Place in Rocky Point, which all got their starts in 1928. So many of these places — Melvin's in Elizabethtown, since 1938, and The Roast Grill in Raleigh, making the same style of hot dog since 1940 — are, simply, unchanged. And that's why we love them so.

Mustard, chili, slaw, and onions. The method becomes a ritual. The ritual grows into a tradition. The tradition turns into legacy. Simple, easy, and everlasting. **OS**

Working Waters

A tour aboard a shrimp trawler in Sneads Ferry sheds light on what it means to make a living on the water.

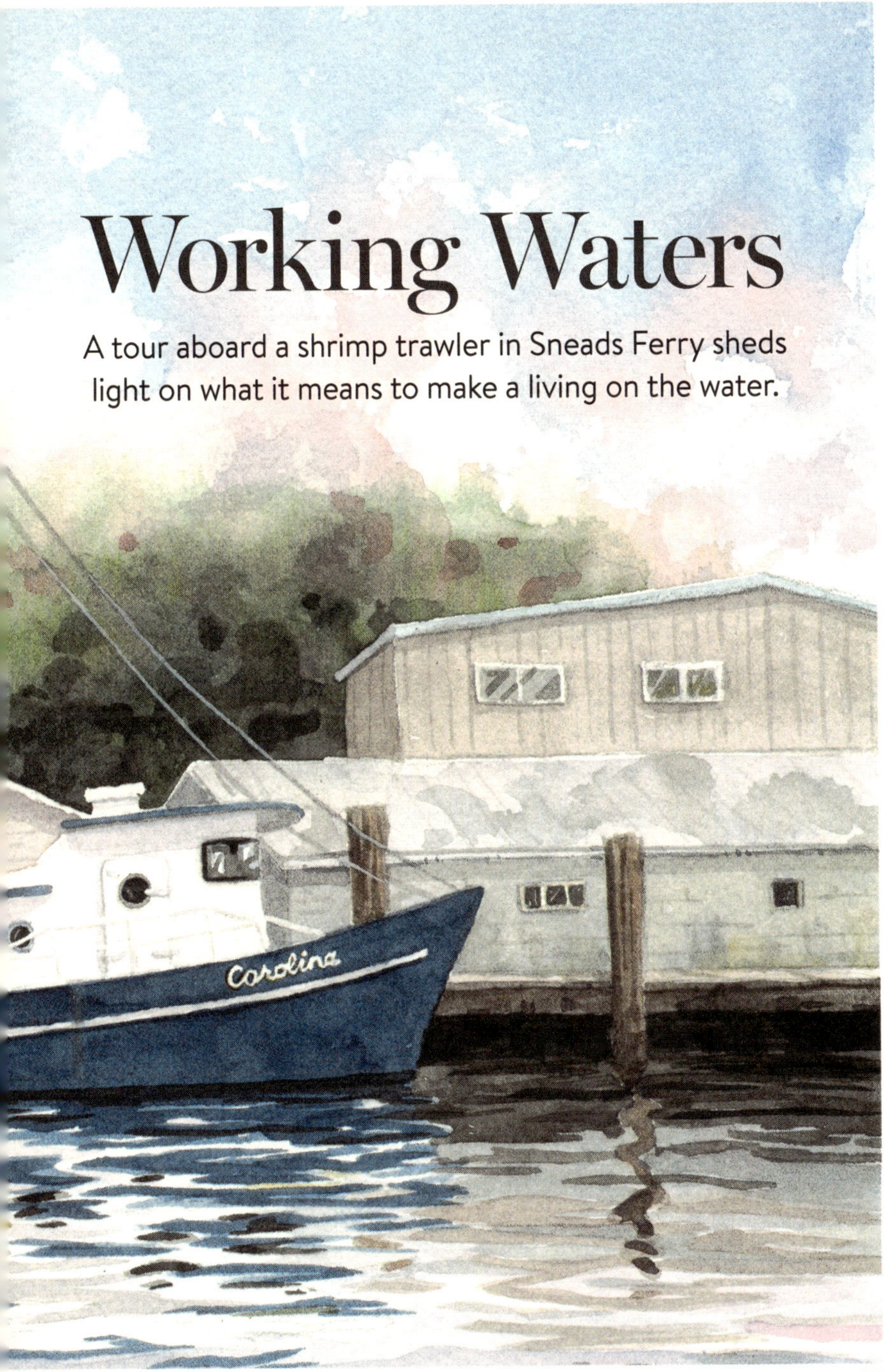

Capt. Tommie Jarman handed me a pair of "Sneads Ferry sneakers," or white rubber boots — rubber so that I wouldn't slip on the wet deck of the boat; white so that I wouldn't leave scuff marks — and I climbed aboard his 35-foot wooden shrimp trawler named *Faith & Hope*.

Captain Jarman runs Reel Livin' Fishing Charters in Sneads Ferry, a small fishing village on the New River in Onslow County that's been christened the "Shrimp Capital of the East Coast" and is home to the North Carolina Shrimp Festival. Only about 2,700 people live here year-round, and judging from the number of trawlers and fishing boats I saw outside of Davis Seafood, outside of Mitchell's Seafood, outside of Grant's Oyster House, I'd say it's a safe bet that there are far more shrimp here than people.

If you live here, you likely have a boat, and I saw plenty of skiffs, sun-battered dinghies, and charters painted with appropriate names: *Knot Today, Shells and Tails, Just a Fluke.*

I stood in awe of the people who make up our fishing industry, the ones who operate the boats and ply the waters.

I've been a passenger on a few North Carolina boats over the years — Capt. Dale Britt's *Sensation*, boat-builder Jarrett Bay's first custom boat;

Capt. Steve Bishop's 45-foot catamaran in Beaufort; Capt. Scott Martin's water taxi on the Lockwood Folly River — pleasure cruises all, but this was the first one where I got to do some work. I was aboard Captain Jarman's boat to learn firsthand what goes into netting a haul of shrimp, what it means to make a living on the water.

I grew up in Randolph County, 175 miles inland from any kind of shrimping. The closest body of water was Lake Lucas, home to catfish and crappie, and the closest thing to fresh seafood I knew was the fried flounder platter at Sea King Fish Camp or the broiled trout at Back Creek. During my three-hour tour with Captain Jarman, I watched him work, gauging our location for the best catch; maneuvering the hydraulics that lower the antennae-like outriggers; hooking nets; clipping pulleys and cables; raising nets and funneling the load of slippery shrimp onto the boat, where I understood, gratefully, why I was wearing those rubber boots.

When I say that I "did some work," I mean that Captain Jarman let me put on a pair of thick sorting gloves to help filter the shrimp from crabs and other fish, and he took my picture holding our surprise catch — a sheepshead! — that made its way into the net. Which is to say that I did nothing at all other than stand in awe of the people, like Captain Jarman, who make up our fishing industry, the ones who operate the boats and run the charters and ply the waters and support these coastal communities and give our state an economic backbone on which we can all shoulder so much pride.

At the end of our run, as the sun lowered and the water shimmered, Captain Jarman dropped me off at the marina, my cooler full of fresh shrimp, my heart full of admiration for these fishermen and -women, and my appreciation as deep as the briny sea. **OS**

Fine Days of Fine Dining

I don't recall such a thing as a "children's menu" in the 1970s, not one that my parents ever pointed out to me, at least.

At restaurants, I ordered from the main menu and ate what everyone else ate: a fried flounder platter at Sea King Fish Camp, a chopped barbecue sandwich at Blue Mist Bar-B-Q, a vegetable plate with fried okra and macaroni and cheese (counts as a vegetable, right?) at Dixie Restaurant. In Asheboro, meals out were at familiar spots, the food not so different than what my mom or grandmother would've cooked at home: meatloaf, country-style steak, chicken pie.

But on the occasional Saturday night, my dad would put on a sport coat and my mom would brush the tangles out of my hair, and the three of us would head to Pinewood Country Club for dinner.

As much as I loved going out to eat — for the Royal Feast at Sir Pizza or the baked spaghetti at Apple House Cafeteria or a grilled cheese at Mayberry — those meals were casual, without ceremony. An evening at Pinewood felt like something special.

I remember my dad pulling open the heavy front door and my mom and me, in our nice dresses, walking down the carpeted hallway like we were on a runway. The hall led past the bar, its wall made out of wavy glass blocks, backlit and glowing gold. I'd cup my hands on the cool blocks and try to see through, catching the prismatic view of the gleaming brass rack above the bar that held wine glasses, their reflections glinting like diamonds.

On past the room where we hung up our coats, and then we were in the dining room, chandeliers sparkling overhead, and on each table, a white tablecloth and candles with tiny silver shades and cloth napkins that had been folded into perfect pyramids.

I couldn't get enough of those napkins, and I was ecstatic when my grandmother saved a *Good Housekeeping* article with a napkin-folding tutorial so I could practice this fanciness at home.

At the table, someone pulled out my mom's chair for her; someone clapped my dad on the shoulder and asked about his golf game. And at some point, a smiling server placed in front of me, with a grand flourish, my favorite thing, the only thing I ever remember eating at Pinewood: shrimp cocktail in a glass bowl on a bed of ice, a tiny fork to eat it with, a ring of cocktail sauce right in the center.

When I think back to my first introduction to a special-occasion meal, I think of the three of us.

I've since dined at many fine places in North Carolina — the elegant McNinch House in Charlotte and Il Palio Ristorante in Chapel Hill; the exquisite Fearrington House Restaurant in Pittsboro and Kimball's Kitchen in Duck. I spent my birthday at Saint Jacques in Gibsonville. At every place, I've appreciated the experience as much as the food.

But when I think back to the place that gave me my first introduction to a special-occasion meal, I think of my dad proclaiming his medium-rare steak excellent, and my mom delighting over the silver boat of blue-cheese dressing, and the three of us enjoying an out-of-the-ordinary moment, a night to remember.

School of Thought

We thought it was a privilege to get tapped on the shoulder by the teacher and then handed those dry, dusty, dirty chalkboard erasers. Two of us were chosen, then sent outside to clap the erasers clean, which we did by pounding them with all our third-grade might against the red-brick wall of the school building, pummeling out rectangular smudges of powder, leaving ghost tracings on the wall, plumes of pulverized chalk clouding the air, coating our hands.

It was an honor to be called up to the board — to write out a spelling word, to work out a math problem, or, before the last bell rang, to be part of the team that got to wash down the chalkboard, plunging a rag into a bucket of water to wipe away the remnants of the day, in preparation to start fresh tomorrow.

The chalkboard was the focal point of the classroom, the canvas on which everything meaningful was laid out for us. A penmanship chart mounted just above it reminded us how to form a perfect cursive curl at the top of a capital D or T; a daily tally in the corner of the board told us who had sold the most World's Finest Chocolate bars; a name with a check mark noted who among us was talking too much. We were riveted to it every day, its place in the hierarchy of importance second only to the American flag hanging from a pole in the corner and to which we pledged allegiance every morning.

> **It was such a surprise, a gift I hadn't even known I'd wanted.**

When I wasn't in school, I played school, retreating to my room with my own chalkboard on a folding wooden easel. Store-bought chalk was never as smooth as school chalk — there was a grittiness to my Crayola chalk, but that didn't stop me from carefully forming my name in the corner — "Miss Hudson" — and assigning lessons to my attentive, if eclectic, class of students: Mrs. Beasley, Holly Hobbie, Stretch Armstrong, Ballerina Barbie.

Eventually, my chalkboard migrated to the bedroom closet, along with my dolls, and then to the attic, and then out of the house altogether, a clean removal, an inevitable clearing away.

After my school years, I didn't think about chalkboards anymore, schoolroom relics supplanted by other mediums of communication — loose-leaf notepaper and spiral notebooks, then word processors, and, finally, thin laptops and phones that fit in our palms: handheld, modern slates for taking notes, typing messages, recording our days, our lives.

And then: Several years ago, I came home from work to find that my dad had been at my house, where he'd built and bolted, onto my fence, a chalkboard, 5-feet-wide by 3-feet-tall, a wooden frame around it that he'd painted a tranquil turquoise.

It was such a surprise, a gift I hadn't even known I'd wanted. He'd written "Love, Dad" on it, a message that has long since been erased by wind and rain, but I still know that it was there.

The chalkboard went with me when I moved to my townhouse. It's affixed to my patio fence now, where I can see it from my window. Every week, I write a new message — quotes from writers I like, poems, itineraries for trips I want to take. Messages visible only to me, and to the birds, and to the open air, the sky, and the heavens. **Os**

Summer's Last Stand

As a kid in the South, making the most of steamy late summer is all about keeping your cool.

By August, we'd surrendered, succumbed to the steam and swelter of a late Southern summer, and no amount of frozen Zero candy bars doled out at the Memorial Park swimming pool in Asheboro could cool us down. We hotfooted around that concrete deck, bouncing on tiptoes to keep from scorching our heels, before diving into water that had gone lukewarm, until we finally just gave up, headed home, and retreated to the backyard, a place where we could still find respite from the baking heat. There, we could lounge beneath the outstretched limbs of a black walnut tree, like the one I sprawled under at my grandmother's house, spreading out one of her quilts to shield my bare legs against the prickle of the brittle grass. If you were in the east, maybe you found your relief under the broad, five-lobed leaves — a giant's hand — of a massive sycamore; if you were in the west, maybe under the canopy of a white oak, the venerable fixture shading an old homeplace.

If the first part of summer was to embrace warmth — at the beach, at a pool, our faces turned toward the sun — the second half of summer was to let it go.

We said our goodbyes to the beach, pocketing seashells to bring home and line up on the windowsill as proof that we'd been somewhere. We watched honeysuckle and magnolia and confederate jasmine and purple irises bloom and then fade. The strawberries were long gone and the soft-shell crabs were dwindling, but there were still plenty of tomatoes for sandwiches, still peaches and watermelon, shockingly cold eaten straight from the refrigerator. Instead

If the first part of summer was to embrace warmth, the second half was to let it go.

of welcoming the heat, we chased the chill. We made creamy icebox pies with lemons and buttermilk and ate cold salads for supper: chicken, shrimp, three-bean, macaroni, potato. We sat for hours in front of the fan, the kind with metal blades, talking into it, making robot voices, for our afternoon entertainment.

We jumped at the chance to make one last right-before-school-starts trip to Carowinds, where we rode the Powder Keg Log Flume over and over, just to be drenched with water at the end of the ride.

On Sundays, we climbed into the back seat of the car for a ride along the Blue Ridge Parkway, all of the windows rolled down, arms brandished out and waving in mountain air that felt 15 degrees cooler than back home. We stood under waterfalls, no longer bone-shatteringly icy but at last just right. We ducked underground into the cooling caves of Linville Caverns. We took to the trails and sought out creeks and streams, stripping off our shoes and socks to wade, to splash in the cool water before the season was over, before it would be time, in a few months, to wish for warmth. *Os*

Back to Basics

In the early morning hours, before school, I could hear the low thunder of the logging trucks, the 18-wheelers, the tractor trailers, hauling their loads of tree-length timber to McDowell Lumber, the sawmill just down the road from my house on Old Highway 49 in Asheboro. The trucks carried poplar, red oak, and white oak, bare-limbed and cut into 50-foot lengths, perfectly stacked onto the beds like toothpicks.

Those logs were on their way to becoming cabinets and doors, furniture and floors. In fact, the floors in the house where I grew up were cut from white oak trees, hewn right on our property when the house was built and then milled for us at McDowell's. Every morning, I'd pad down the stairs and across those floors, sleepyheaded and barefooted, to the breakfast table, a solid oak piece like the floors, that my parents found in a High Point antiques shop in 1973. I'd slide out my chair — solid ash, made for us by Boling Furniture in Siler City — my dad already at the table with his coffee, my mom in the kitchen, slicing bananas for her bowl of Special K. I ate Pop-Tarts or chocolate Carnation breakfast bars and drank Tang, choices that are unthinkable to me now. My adult tastes evolved to pastured eggs and whole-wheat toast and real fruit rather than my beloved Fruity Pebbles and Apple Jacks, which, to my

knowledge, contained no actual apples.

It's funny how things — tastes, styles — change over time, and there was plenty of artificiality in the world I knew back then: We replaced my metal lunch box with plastic Tupperware; my friends and I filled our mouths with Pop Rocks and sucked colored syrup made from Lord-knows-what out of wax bottles. By the eighth grade, I was learning to shadow my eyes with unnatural shades of powder blues and neon purples. My grandmother put aside her cotton dresses in favor of polyester pantsuits. My dad built a gazebo inside my mom's crafts shop in the Randolph Mall so she could stock faux flowers — silk and nylon — for wreaths and floral arrangements.

Such were the times.

Eventually, as they always do, the classics returned. Farmers markets have popped up everywhere in North Carolina. People have embraced gardening, canning, pickling, and preserving once again. Back to basics. The old ways made new. Our Tupperware got packed away, and it's been a long time since I peeled back the foil on a TV dinner. These days, when I have supper with my mom — meatloaf made from scratch; a homemade banana pudding — I slide a chair back from the table, one of those same Boling Furniture chairs that I've always known. Now, though, I sit in the one that was my dad's, not quite filling the space he left, but comfortable in knowing that the wood is still as solid and strong as the day it was built. **OS**

Eventually, as they always do, the classics returned. The old ways made new.

Places of the Heart

In 1990, my mom closed the crafts shop she'd owned for 20 years and took a job as a salesperson at Rhodes Furniture in Greensboro. She'd never sold furniture before, and it was the first time she'd worked for someone else since waitressing as a teenager in the '60s. It had to have been hard, a change like that, but my mom embraced it.

Rhodes carried several North Carolina-manufactured lines of furniture — Broyhill, Klaussner, Thomasville, Kincaid — but my mom's favorite was the Bob Timberlake collection, then made by Lexington Furniture. She was drawn to the Arts and Crafts style, which complemented the antiques already in our house, and my dad loved the look, too. When the Timberlake Gallery opened in Lexington in the mid-'90s, my parents were some of the first people at the opening. They made a day of it, having lunch at the Bar-B-Q Center, popping into the shops on Main Street, and picking up a bag of Red Bird Sticks at The Candy Factory to eat in the car on the way home. They spent their afternoon browsing furniture.

At the showroom, my mom swooned over a solid cherry poster bed, so rich and warm, and with her earnings from her new job, she bought it. After years of sleeping on my great-grandmother's handed-down wrought-iron bed, my parents were excited to bring home something new, something that belonged to them alone.

For a moment, I got a glimpse of how my mom and dad must've spent their days together.

She kept working, driving from Asheboro to Greensboro every day, putting in hours on holidays and weekends, and when she could afford more, she bought more — adding nightstands, a gentleman's chest of drawers, a pottery hutch in the dining room. My dad accompanied her on every trip, and Lexington became *their* place: lunch together, shops on Main Street, candy or ice cream at the end of the day.

I've thought of the two of them often

when I travel around North Carolina — how my dad, with his artistic eye, loved to look at window displays; how my mom, with her furniture knowledge, could spot a good antique; how they both had a sweet tooth and ended the day with a treat. I never went along with them; those days belonged to them alone.

A couple of months ago, for my birthday, my mom and I took a trip to Blowing Rock. It was a beautiful day for walking, and we spent our time shopping on Main Street, admiring the window displays. We picked up a slice of fudge from Kilwins to share on the ride home. For a moment, I got a glimpse of how my mom and dad must've spent their days together.

For lunch, we headed over to Chetola Resort, to Timberlake's Restaurant. My mom had never been there, and, well, I wish you could've seen her face when we walked in. The restaurant is filled with that Timberlake furniture so familiar to her, tables and chairs in the same solid oak and cherry that she'd filled our house with. I could see how much it reminded her of the beautiful home that she and my dad had created.

We chose a table next to the fireplace, overlooking the lake. My mom pointed to the wooden beams on the ceiling — "just like what we had in our den," she reminded me, her voice carrying her back to another place.

We ate our fish-and-chips and watched the resident swans, the male and the female named Moses and Bertha, the ones who've settled here on this beautiful lake, a place that seems to belong to them alone. **OS**

Seaside Shangri-Las

It's easy to escape to another era at a classic coastal retreat.

What a grand time it must've been at Kitty Hawk, at Kill Devil Hills, at Nags Head back in the day, before there were flashing neon "Vacancy" signs, before the four-lane bypass was built parallel to the Beach Road, before the motel billboards touted color television and free HBO. The Sea Ranch — you know the one, oceanfront on the Outer Banks, adorned with the curving, azure seahorse on the side of the building — held weekly cocktail parties hosted by the owner, Alice Sykes. Story goes that Alice was instrumental in introducing liquor by the drink to Dare County and likely sold the first mixed drink on the island. (How I would love to know what that drink was!) Guests were known to flock to the Sea Ranch for Alice's elaborately themed parties — and her homemade crab bisque.

What a glorious time it must've been to watch so many beach motels spring up 60 years ago, 70 years ago: the Tan-A-Rama Motel next to the Avalon Pier, recognizable for the sky blue window shutters; the Beacon Motor Lodge; the Vacationer; the Vivianna; the Sea Oatel and Dareolina Restaurant, all family-owned places with names that flirted with frivolity and gaiety, promising icy-cold air-conditioning and mom-and-pop warmth.

I'm sorry these places didn't last, enduring only in memory now, victims of hurricanes or erosion or perhaps modern progress.

But I can still get a sense of what a bright and breezy time it must've been at the 1960s-era Atlantis Lodge in Pine Knoll Shores, which has held on to its history so completely, its modernist architecture still intact, its live-oak landscaping thriving through generations of care.

These legacy places on our coast are retreats in every sense of the word.

It's a small thing, but I get a thrill when I'm handed the room key — an actual metal key, not a plastic card — dangling from its rhombus-shaped keychain, mid-century geometry in the palm of my hand, and open the door to the room with its retro furniture, its white tulip table, its polished sliding-glass doors overlooking an ocean view that's immutable, unchanging, ageless.

And I can still feel what it must've been like at the Blockade Runner in Wrightsville Beach, which propels me right into 1964, when the hotel was built. The lobby is modernized now, with an undulating tiled ceiling and tropical murals and shiny metal fish sculptures on the walls, but the mood is still swanky, the structure — the bones — still intact.

These legacy places on our coast — the classic First Colony Inn and the Sea Foam Motel in Nags Head, both on the National Register of Historic Places; The Cavalier by the Sea in Kill Devil Hills, which still has its original knotty pine paneling on the walls of the rooms and clotheslines strung beneath the eaves to dry bathing suits — are retreats in every sense of the word. They are our vacation escapes, yes, but they also offer a retreat to another era, an ebb away.

Long may they stand. **OS**

The Best Seat in the House

The chair was a soft cornflower blue, velvet with a button-tufted back, made in Lenoir by the Fairfield Chair Company, which, 50 years ago, had already been making chairs for 50 years, so I think they knew what they were doing.

That chair swiveled and rocked, and although it was made for one person, my grandmother was slender and didn't take up much room. And I was small, 6 years old, so I didn't either, and the two of us fit perfectly in that chair together, filling in all the space, she on the right side, loose Kleenex tissues stashed in between the arm and the seat cushion; me wedged on the left side, feet barely reaching the ottoman in front of us.

In winter, when school was out for the holidays, when it was too cold to work in the garden and too cold to walk to the neighbors' and too cold to sit on the front porch in another set of chairs — her cane-back Kennedy Rockers from P&P Chair Company; the factory was just a few blocks from her house — my grandmother turned on the television and she and I wriggled ourselves into that chair in the den, settling in to watch her stories, as she called them, daytime soaps, first with *All My Children* right after lunch, then *As the World Turns* and *Guiding Light*. I tried to take in what I could of the storylines — by the time I was a freshman at Appalachian State University, some 12 years later, those stories had somehow become my stories, too; I knew Pine Valley and Springfield as well as I knew Asheboro, and I scheduled my classes around the timing of *General Hospital* — but mostly, back then, I was happy just to sit next to my grandmother, shoulder to shoulder, while we watched TV and she worked on a needlepoint piece, her eyes darting from the needle and yarn in her lap to the screen.

Even now, I can't remember ever feeling quite so warm, quite so content.

She made large tapestries — wall samplers and covers for her organ bench and footstools — and her canvases, stitched with heavy Persian wool, draped across our legs like a blanket while she worked. My head nodded as we rocked and my eyes fell closed as I watched her pull those stitches slowly and rhythmically. Even now, I can't remember ever feeling quite so warm; I can't remember ever feeling quite so content.

Years later, after my grandfather died — he had his own chair where he'd sit in the evenings and listen to Cronkite tell us the way it was — and my grandmother moved from their house to an assisted-living apartment, the Fairfield chair went with her, pressing against the walls of her new, smaller den, and although I didn't try to squeeze in with her anymore, the chair dwarfed her, her narrow shoulders gone a bit slighter, her lean legs gone a bit thinner.

On weekends, when I'd visit, I'd find her in the chair, her hands empty and folded in her lap, arthritis having long stopped the needlepoint, but she'd always swivel the chair toward me when I walked in the room, rocking and smiling, and I'd find a way to sit as close as I could.

When my grandmother couldn't sit in the chair anymore, we helped her up and eased her into the bed, a more comfortable spot. You know, it takes a rocking chair a few seconds to stop after someone exits from it. I'd never noticed that until the day that I did.

Occasionally these days, when I stop by an estate sale on a Saturday, I'll run across one of those old chairs, one that looks exactly like my grandmother's, even if the velvet is a spring green instead of blue, even if the armrests look a bit more worn. I wonder for a minute who sat there, whether they had a grandchild of their own, someone who found a way to stay close, to climb in and fill the empty space. **Os**

Miracle on Fayetteville Street

In 2019, a new business opened at 156 South Fayetteville Street in downtown Asheboro — a gourmet popcorn shop called Asheboro Popcorn Co. — and the owners had the place looking so good. They put up a red-and-white-striped — cherry red, Christmas red — awning and painted the front door to match. They propped red-and-white-striped pillows in the front window and built the tables and counter by hand from local white oak.

Inside, on the wall, they framed an old paper menu, yellowed with age and stained with grease spatters and, well ... give me just a minute on that.

Years before this space became a popcorn shop, it housed the Recreation Soda Shop. My dad worked there in the 1950s, when he was in high school, pulling Cokes and dipping ice cream. He went off to college, the soda shop changed hands a time or two, and then, in 1979, my dad bought the equipment in the old restaurant — the milkshake machine and ice cream freezer, the flattop grill, the bun steamer, all of it — and opened his own sandwich shop in the same spot called Phil's, his first name.

He worked so hard to make the place special. He built the seating by hand, booths from local white pine. He painted the front door and hung wallpaper, an herb pattern, and boxed up utensils from our kitchen at home — spatulas, spoons, and forks — and carted them to the restaurant. He used my mom's stockpots for his vegetable soup. He chopped pounds of chicken for chicken salad and grated piles of Cheddar for his pimento cheese.

And he wrote a four-page menu, typing every word on my beloved red — cherry red, Christmas red — Smith-Corona manual typewriter. I sat beside him at the kitchen table, helping him hunt for the letters as he pecked out descriptions for his country ham sandwich (*"from Watauga County and not too salty"*) and his famous footlong hot dog (*"Bryan's best all-meat wiener"*). His restaurant drew a crowd — lawyers

He wrote a four-page menu, typing every word on my beloved red Smith-Corona manual typewriter.

and bankers and downtown shoppers came in every day — and for years, my dad helped feed a town.

It had been 40 years since Phil's closed when I got a note from the new tenants, the popcorn shop folks, a husband-and-wife named Greg and Sara Holden. In the process of redesigning the space, Sara told me, they'd uncovered something wedged behind an old cabinet that she thought I'd want to know about.

I drove to Asheboro to visit the shop — first time I'd been in the space in 40 years. Sara and Greg had renovated it beautifully. I saw the cheerful red awning, the red door, and then, there, framed on the wall, well ... give me just a minute on this.

There it was, that old menu typed so carefully by my dad, now hung in a place of honor by people who never knew his restaurant, but who felt a kinship for what came before, for the memories housed in this space. My face wet with tears, I read every word again. My dad would've been so happy to see it all, to know that something he created had endured, preserved in a space filled with stories and history, infused with so much cheer and joy. What a wonderful gift. **OS**

Artist Laura Poss, a North Carolina native, began drawing at a young age and has been making art ever since. Today, watercolor is her medium of choice, and her work has been exhibited throughout the state and across the country. She currently lives with her husband in Greensboro. See more at lauraposs.com.